RADI8

Radi8

*Using the Practice of Yoga to
Cultivate Your Inner Shine*

Sindy Warren

Printed in the United States of America

First, printing 2018
Cover design by Lindsay Flack

ISBN-13: 978-1-947637-33-7 print edition
ISBN-13: 978-1-947637-34-4 ebook edition

Waterside Press 2055
Oxford Ave Cardiff,
CA 92007
www.waterside.com

For Olivia
May you be happy
May you be healthy
May you be safe
May you walk through
the world with ease

TABLE OF CONTENTS

Be yourself. Everyone else is already taken.

—Oscar Wilde

INTRODUCTION

Rumor has it that when someone once asked Michelangelo how he created his most famous statue, David, he responded, "I didn't create David, as he was already there. All I did was chip away at the parts of the stone that weren't him."

So too, this book is about the ancient practice of yoga and how it can help us cultivate our own sense of Michelangelo as a pathway to finding our inner David. We all have a best self and yet most of us are not living that version of ourselves, at least not much of the time. However, through the practice of yoga and all that it entails, we can become more open to shed that which doesn't serve us; that which isn't really us at all. When we focus on our practice we can get closer to being the best we can possibly be. And to me, being our best selves and sharing that with the world around us is perhaps one of the best answers to the eternal question each of us faces: "Why am I here?"

Modern yoga can at times seem to be concerned almost exclusively with physical postures that are known to increase flexibility and muscular tone. We think of a "yoga body" as one that is lean and long. However, the practice of yoga goes far beyond the physical. In fact the physical practice of yoga, or *asana* as it's called in the ancient language of Sanskrit, is only a very small aspect of yoga. What, then, is a larger understanding of yoga?

Yoga comes from the Sanskrit *"yuj,"* which means to yoke, or stated differently, to unite. An interpretation that really speaks to me is that yoga is all about connection. Finding that place where the separation between you and me is bridged. Where we acknowledge our shared humanity and view our world and one another through a deep-looking lens. According to the *Yoga Sutras*, widely considered the preeminent text in yoga philosophy, yoga is a journey containing eight separate and interrelated parts, or limbs. This path provides us with answers on how to live our best lives, decrease suffering in the world, and find enlightenment. Consider the number eight itself, which represents the classic eight-part path of yoga. Can you picture it in your mind's eye? Now turn it on its side. It's an infinity sign, a symbol of connection and oneness—this, along with other understanding, leads to the very essence of yoga.

In addition to denoting connection, yoga is a physical practice; it is meditation, it is mindfulness, it is breath awareness and control, and it is a philosophy rooted in Eastern tradition. And that's just for starters. Though awareness of these life-changing benefits is increasing, the richness of the yoga practice is still largely a well-kept secret in America. In fact, fewer than 10 percent of Americans practice yoga today, however the good news is this is a big increase over the amount of those who practiced it 20 years ago.

And among those practicing now, thousands of these "yogis" have no idea that the fabric of yoga extends far, far beyond the sticky mat at their local yoga studio. Many are under the impression that being "advanced" at yoga means being able to place their foot behind their head or stand on their hands. While these are examples of advanced physical postures, they represent only a slice of the whole of yoga. So what I mean to say is that adeptness at postural prowess does not necessarily indicate significant advancement on the yoga path.

This book is for anyone who practices yoga, is considering practicing yoga, or is simply yoga-curious. It is less about the physical aspects of yoga and more about how its ancient roots provide modern yogis with accessible tools to live our best lives. Touching your toes or standing on your head is not required.

First, above all, yoga is a practice that is all-inclusive where everyone is welcome. It is open to men, women, and children of all races, religions, body shapes and sizes, and socioeconomic status. If you have a willing heart and an open mind, I am confident you will find something along the path that speaks to you deeply.

How I Found My Way to the Mat

Yoga and I flirted a little bit before we began going steady. I went to a class or two after I had sprained my ankle running, circa 2001, thinking it would be therapeutic. I was working as a lawyer in Cleveland at the time and was about as tightly wound and "Type A" as you can imagine, just like many of my colleagues. I had gone to competitive schools and had worked at high-pressure law firms in San Francisco, Boston and Cleveland.

The "work hard" ethos is what I grew up with. So it is no surprise that as an adult I worked hard. I worked out hard mostly every day, equally to relieve stress and burn calories, as much as to keep up with always being on the go. Like everyone I knew at the time, I had no idea yoga was anything other than stretching and light exercise. Suffice it to say I was unimpressed with the class. It didn't seem strenuous enough and I didn't know what the heck I was doing most of the class. Turns out I was dead wrong on the first count and spot on with the second.

A couple of years later, pregnant and living in Boston, I went to a handful of prenatal yoga classes. Again, the whole experience struck me as "meh." I did not get the point of the physical moves and I did not find any inspiration. I just hoped the classes would help when it came time for the big push (can't say that they did, though I really had no idea what I was doing either in class or in childbirth).

When my daughter was a few months old in 2003, I was back in Cleveland and found my way to a nearby studio where I began to practice in earnest. Unlike before, my passion arose this time because I experienced yoga in an entirely new way. As the Buddhist proverb says, "when the student is ready, the teacher will appear." Yoga was my teacher, and I was ready for school.

What first grabbed me was the sheer physicality of it all. The delight I felt was, I imagine, something akin to what it felt like when I first learned to walk. Moving my body in totally new ways, finding physical expression that I had never before experienced was magical. And the breath! The simple synchronization of breath and movement—who knew this could feel so damn good?

So I soon got into a routine of practicing several times a week. Religiously. I didn't feel quite right if I missed a day or, god forbid, a week. My body craved the movement of the physical practice. My mind soon followed suit, wanting the sense of clarity and calm that often resulted. I didn't understand why I felt so drawn to yoga, but I listened to my body and mind (and heart and soul) and came back again and again.

By nature, I am extremely impatient. I used to honk at the car in front of me if the light had just one second before turned green and the driver had yet to step on the gas. My apologies if you ever happened to be in front of me. This impatience is probably very closely related, in an emotional hardwired kind of way, to my general inclination towards reactivity. We all have a kind of "set point" when it comes to reactivity.

If provoked or annoyed in some way, how quick are you to respond? Is your anger slow to simmer but dangerous once it does? Or are your outbursts more of the instantaneous kind? Or neither—if so, are you sure you're alive?

I tend toward the quick trigger kind of reactivity. Actually I mean to write that in the past tense "tended toward" because, I swear it's true, yoga has slowed me down in many ways. I've long said that one of the most significant changes I've experienced as a yogi is the ability to cultivate space between stimulus and response. As Austrian neurologist and psychologist Victor Frankl wrote in *Man's Search for Ultimate Meaning*, "Between stimulus and response there is a space. In that space is our power to choose our response. In our response lies our growth and our freedom." Thus, I've come to know intimately that yoga is more than just a form of exercise. It's a philosophy, art, and science dating back more than five thousand years, that offers big answers to our biggest questions.

Here's an example. When I was in my mid-twenties I developed a pretty debilitating eating disorder; I binged. I would binge uncontrollably but never purge. For a couple of years I didn't even know what I had had a name—it was way different from the more commonly known bulimia or anorexia. I just assumed something was terribly wrong with me. I was able to overcome my disorder after a few years thanks to the wonderful support of my husband and that of a great therapist, but the scars still remained. Truth be told, they'll probably always be a part of me.

Yet my yoga practice has evolved to become an incredible soothing balm for these scars. I don't think it's an exaggeration to say yoga changed my chemistry. What used to be an incessant stream of self-flagellating thoughts has transformed into a comforting current of self-acceptance. Not all the time of course, but a lot of the time. That is the power of the practice. It can transform us, heal us, and help us grow into our potential. Some would say the practice of yoga does not transform us into something new. Rather, it restores us to the beautiful souls we were to begin with. Thus, Michelangelo hewing closer to David.

One of the guiding principles of yoga that has had the most impact on me is to be centered and grounded, not susceptible to the vicissitudes of daily life. Imagine a tree with many branches. When the wind blows, the branches sway. But how much they sway depends on the wind. And the tree. Now we can't control the winds in our lives. However, we can work on developing ourselves into the kind of tree that has a sturdy trunk and solid branches.

With respect to a wind gusting from waiting too long at a traffic light, or a wind gusting from telling yourself over and over again that you suck, we want to be a solid enough tree that we're not thrown off kilter. Now when something bigger happens, like the loss of a loved one or really any kind of heartache, don't expect or even strive to have still, unmoving branches. Rather, hope to have enough of a grounding and sense of self to survive the storm—to be standing when the grief subsides. That's my hope for myself, anyway, and for you. And I think yoga has a lot to teach us about how to become that steady, rooted person, just like the metaphorical tree I have described.

I had developed and sustained a serious yoga practice for well over a decade before I ever considered teaching yoga. Now that I am a yoga and meditation teacher, I can barely remember what life was like before. It's been an absolutely joyous part of my own journey and I consider it a deep honor to share my knowledge about yoga with others.

While I've laid out an overview of what I mean by the term "yoga," I'd like to add that yoga can be, well, not much in the way of how most traditionally picture yoga. Take my husband as an example. He does not often take my yoga classes, or anyone else's. He eschews Downward-facing Dog and just about any other pose you can name. He does not read books on yoga philosophy. He knows no Sanskrit. Yet, he has a quality of calmness and non-reactivity about him that soothes my soul.

So yoga can take many forms. You may never make it to a studio or unroll a sticky mat, however you can still be engaged in the pursuit of yoga. Though this book is focused on the more traditional parts of yoga, it is my hope that some form of the practice will speak to you on a deep level and will infiltrate your life in a way that brings you equanimity, peace, and joy. Yoga has done that for me. I am privileged to pay it forward.

The Eight Limbs

According to scholars, the yoga tradition began in India more than 5,000 years ago. It involved a systematic approach to living life with knowledge, wisdom, and mastery over the mind as a way to deal with the condition of being human. Much like the Talmud in the Jewish faith, it was passed on verbally from teacher to student, generation after generation. The first comprehensive presentation of yoga philosophy, the *Yoga Sutras*, was compiled by the sage Patanjali sometime between 500 and 200 BC. The Sutras is a collection of 195 aphorisms or "threads" that set forth the eight-limbed path of yoga, its philosophy, and practice.

Sanskrit is one of the oldest languages on earth and considered the traditional language of yoga. The word "Sanskrit" means refined, perfect or polished, which is an apt way to describe the goal of the practice of yoga. You'll see Sanskrit terms throughout this book, as the current use of Sanskrit is considered a nod of respect to the practice's historical underpinnings.

I mentioned that the sweaty physical practice that happens in a yoga studio, or that's displayed in Instagram glamour shots of friends of friends in pretzel-like contortions, is really just a small part of this thing called yoga. To be precise, it is only one of the eight limbs, and not even the first or second. Here is an overview on the limbs:

1. *Yamas*: behavior restraints, code of ethics to be observed, or how we act in relation to our world
2. *Niyamas*: internal positive restraints, or how we act in relation to ourselves
3. *Asana*: the physical postures
4. *Pranayama*: breathing exercises, breath control, vital energy
5. *Pratyahara*: sense withdrawal or sensory inhibition
6. *Dharana*: concentration
7. *Dhayana*: meditation
8. *Samadhi*: enlightenment

Sounds pretty esoteric, right? If you dig in a little deeper though, it's actually an extremely relevant blueprint for living your best life. I know that's a lofty claim. So let me be clear: I'm not suggesting this path called yoga is a magic happy pill or that it will deliver some kind of perfect life. It's not, and it won't. But what it can do is help clarify what's really important to you, shed what's not, and offer guidance to live from a place of your authentic self. And when we live from that place, our inner Davids can shine forth.

Let me add an important caveat. While there are some schools of thought that suggest strict adherence to the eight-limbed path is *the* way, I invite you to be skeptical. This is not a one-size-fits-all "take it or leave it" proposition. See what resonates with you and be wary of what doesn't. The path of yoga, in my mind, is a personal journey, unique to each person, to create for themselves with the benefit of a solid knowledge base and an experienced teacher or two along the way.

Chapter One
The Yamas – Honoring the World Around You

Who are you? I bet if someone you just met asked you that, you would rattle off a bunch of labels. For example, I'm a yoga teacher, a lawyer, a mom, a stepmom, and a wife. This may tell you some of the things I *do* but it doesn't really tell you who I *am*. There are two kinds of relationships that are really at the heart of answering this question: your relationship to the world around you, including but not limited to your nearest and dearest; and your relationship to yourself. Understanding these two can really add contour and definition to your answer.

The yamas are often referred to as "external restraints," as they govern the first of these relationships: how we relate to our world. It can be helpful to think of them as a way to show up in your life with more presence and compassion. There are five of them:

- *Ahimsa* (non-violence)
- *Satya* (truthfulness)
- *Asteya* (non-stealing)

- *Brahmacharya* (non-excess)
- *Aparigraha* (non-possessiveness)

Interpretations abound for these, so remember to use your powers of discernment (*viveka* in Sanskrit) in analyzing how you may want to develop and apply them to your life.

Also, lest you become overwhelmed by the suggestions on how to incorporate these pillars of yoga philosophy, remember that small steps can have a huge impact. In fact, it is through the smallest of actions and choices, seemingly meaningless or not relevant to progress in the moment, that you can make the most significant changes in your life. Perhaps at the end of this chapter you may like to pick one yama to focus on for the next month. Then, move on to another. There are countless ways to begin to live your best life using yoga as your guide. Open your mind and your heart and get ready to play.

- *Ahimsa* (non-violence)

Ahimsa is really at the heart of all yoga philosophy. Do less (or no) harm, be more kind. While ahimsa is usually translated as non-violence, it's far more nuanced than, say, not beating people up. The famous Lao Tzu quote is relevant here:

"Watch your thoughts, for they become words. Watch your words, for they become actions. Watch your actions, for they become habits. Watch your habits, for they become character. Watch your character, for it becomes your destiny."

Ahimsa really does start at the granular level of our thoughts. It certainly extends to our words and of course to our actions. Let's begin with our thoughts. My binge eating disorder involved shoving copious amounts of food into my mouth until I was so sick I literally feared having a heart attack. Then I would make up for my binge by strictly controlling my diet for a few days and exercising a lot, after which I would begin the cycle anew. Because I was so ashamed of and embarrassed by my out of control behavior, I tried to hide my problem, deny it. The result was it took me a long time before I could admit I needed help, and then have the guts to go get it.

Part of the struggle was that my behavior did not fit what I thought an eating disorder looked like. Thus, I concluded I was just hopelessly crazy and not deserving of any degree of compassion. Particularly self-compassion. Man, if you could have seen inside my mind—my mental chatter was incessant and cruel. Words like "hate," "loser," "fat," and "fucked up" seemed to be on an endless loop. Now in hindsight, looking at where I was then through the lens of yoga, it's crystal clear I was violating ahimsa. Yes, ahimsa applies – and indeed, necessarily starts with – ourselves.

The way we talk to ourselves sets the stage for how we show up in our lives. It's an inescapable truth. I could not possibly have hated on myself, day after day, month after month, and even year after year without that affecting how much or how little I was able to give to my loved ones. Or even to waitresses or sales clerks or passersby.

Ironically, the more I lambasted myself in my head, the further I became entrenched in my disordered behavior. It wasn't until I could actually love myself that I could begin to heal. This is such an important point. When we approach ourselves, flaws and all, with ahimsa, we create fertile ground for healing and growth. In case your eyes glazed over there for a sec, let me repeat this—it's that essential:

If you are looking to heal or grow,
you must first learn to love yourself
just as you are.

An anonymous author once said, "You can't punish yourself into change. You can't whip yourself into shape. But you can love yourself into well-being." Wise words.

Let's unpack this whole idea of "self-love" for a moment. It is not an egocentric, "me, me, me" love of which I speak. I would argue, in fact, that arrogant self-regard is not even love at all. Though you would not know that from looking at a lot of our mass media: the "buy this iPhone, Armani, Botox, Netflix, Tesla (it's a never-ending list) and you'll be so happy; everyone will love you and you will love yourself" message constantly bombards us.

But these material possessions never really provide any degree of lasting happiness. We might feel some momentary pleasure, but if we're honest with ourselves, it isn't too long before that craving for more hits again. Why do we fall for this? There's research showing that if you repeat a message enough times, even if it is untruthful, a lot of people will end up believing it. Corporate America's marketing departments do a great job selling us on variations of this same lie again and again—caffè latte, lustrous hair, celebrity—and we are susceptible to believing them.

The ahimsa-based love I suggest you consider cultivating is of a different variety altogether. It is a softer kind of self-acceptance with a sense that you have your own back.

For just a moment close your eyes and imagine what it would feel like to go through your life really feeling like no matter what, you've got your back and you'll be okay. For most of us this would be a radical approach, but that is where practicing ahimsa can take us.

I was married once before, in my late twenties, to my law school sweetheart. When we split just a couple of years into our marriage, I had this kind of gentle, loving attitude towards myself. I readily gave up our home and all of our belongings. To this day I hold on to a very strong memory of telling myself then that I was good so long as I had my big pile of well-loved books and a couple of photo albums: *it's okay, I've got this.* Not coincidentally, at that time I had also begun my journey to heal my binge eating disorder. You see the radical shift I made in the way I was speaking to myself facilitated a new path for healing and growth.

How can we start a loving dialogue with ourselves if we are mired in negative thinking? Positive self-talk, even if it feels forced at first, can do wonders. A simple "I love you," even just inside your head, can begin to counter the terrible damage we inflict on ourselves with our own hurtful words. If that feels too awkward to begin with, then you might want to try "I'm okay" or "I've got this" to start incorporating some helpful self-talk. Meditation with a mantra that denotes love and acceptance is another great tool. Much more on that later.

In the fantastic book *The Yamas and Niyamas,* which I highly recommend for a deeper analysis of these two limbs of the yoga path, author Deborah Adele sums things up well:

> *Our inability to love and accept all pieces of ourselves creates tiny ripples—tiny acts of violence—that have huge and lasting impacts on others.*

When I started to heal from my eating disorder I would still binge, though the interludes between binges grew progressively longer. The biggest change then was the way I spoke to myself after one of my binging episodes. I went from hatefully self-recriminating to compassionately self-forgiving. Back in the day, after I went on a binge, I would hate myself vociferously for several days before I could allow myself to ease up. But as I continued along my path of healing, the forgiveness after a binge began to come sooner. Maybe only a day sooner to begin with. Then two. Then by the end of the same day of my binge. Eventually, I forgave myself pretty much immediately. My inner dialogue went something like this:

> *Self-compassionate me: "Okay so you screwed up again and you feel like crap and tomorrow you'll feel like crap. Oh well, suck it up and move on."*
>
> *Self-hating me: "Why the hell did I binge again? What was I thinking when I ate that first piece of licorice? I knew it would send me screaming for more and then all bets would be off. I'm such a screwed-up idiot! And I'm fat and ugly to boot!"*
>
> *"It's okay, Sindy. You're okay. Just move on and try to do better next time."*
>
> *"But… !!!"*
>
> *"Come on, let it go. You're okay. You can move on and put this behind you. You can do it. Let's go."*
>
> *"Okay if you say so. Thanks."*
>
> *"You're welcome."*

Have you ever actually listened to the voice in your head? The one that tells you you're not enough? Ahimsa asks you to challenge this. Not in a combative way, but in a gentle way, the way you would talk to your best friend or a child you want to comfort.

Ahimsa plays out in our lives in other ways too. For instance, in the words we speak out loud, to and about others. In the ways we treat the earth. In the diets we choose to follow—some yogis insist that you must be a vegan, or at least a vegetarian, to practice ahimsa but I don't agree. While I think foregoing animal products is a wonderful way to engage in ahimsa, as long as we are mindful and discerning in what we choose to consume, we are practicing this yama.

I'll tell you a story related to this. About a decade ago I went from making chicken for dinner three times a week to being a strict vegan. I had read an expose´ on factory farming and immediately decided to eliminate all animal products from my diet. I was extremely disciplined about it for a number of years. Nowadays, while I cook almost exclusively vegan at home, I do eat fish and dairy when I go out. My body feels best when I follow a pescatarian diet. My daughter went through her own metamorphosis. She stopped eating meat when she was four after she made the connection that chicken was, well, chicken, and wanted nothing to do with it. She's never strayed. So too with my stepdaughter, a committed vegetarian. They are, in their own way, practicing ahimsa.

I have a dear yogi friend, also a wonderfully talented yoga teacher, who was a strict vegan for years largely due to spiritual reasons. The lineage of yoga she studied and practiced insists that veganism is an essential ingredient to spiritual growth. My friend adhered to this so strongly that for years she even fed her dog only vegan food.

It turned out her own body would also send her a serious message. Several years ago a doctor whom she greatly respected told her in no uncertain terms that she needed to add meat and fish to her diet in order to be at optimum health. This was a suggestion, though a firm one. He understood that everyone's nutritional needs are unique so his advice was for her and not a generalization for all.

She struggled mightily with this: *would I be compromising my spiritual well-being for my physical health?* Finally, after much soul searching, she began to incorporate humanely-raised animal products into her diet. Her sense of physical well-being and vitality soared. This too was ahimsa.

My friend is still mindful and compassionate about her dietary choices. She balances her belief in non-harming with her desire to feel good in her body. She understands that when she feels her best, she can show up more fully for her loved ones and her yoga students.

I have hurt others, just as you have, just as all people have over the course of a lifetime. Ahimsa asks us to do our part to right our wrongs. And to become so mindful that we really think about those around us and do our best to not hurt their feelings.

I'll tell you a story that has particular meaning to me because it involves people I really care about. An old friend of mine was planning her wedding at the time I was engaged to my first husband. I was the one to introduce my friend to her fiancé, he was also an old friend of mine, and so naturally she asked me to be in the wedding. She was so excited about her marriage, and for good reason in foreseeing their future that became a reality as a great couple with three fantastic kids.

At the time of my friend's wedding, I was also planning my own. Ours was to be the smallest wedding possible without actually eloping: immediate family only. I was also knee-deep in my eating disorder and still largely in denial about it. I was definitely not getting the help I needed. I was also struggling with latent doubts about my own impending nuptials. In short, I was basically a miserable cur.

Thus, instead of being happy for my old friend I was wallowing in self-pity and misery, and as a result felt put out every time we spoke while she was aglow in anticipation of her upcoming milestone. In the back of my mind I knew I was letting her down. In fact I told her I was too busy with my own wedding plans to be able to participate in hers. Yep, I opted out of the bridal party simply because I couldn't really deal. Retelling the story even now literally still makes me cringe.

Years later, after I had gotten my act together in some important ways, I looked back and saw what a complete jerk I had been. I apologized to my old friend, and she forgave me. It took me much longer for me to stop calling myself a jerk and to forgive myself. Nonetheless, I had done some irrevocable damage and had to live with the consequences. Though it did teach me something important. Being so stuck in my head that I cannot be there for others is neither a helpful nor a compassionate way to live. For the most part, I don't live that way anymore.

In thinking about how to apply ahimsa in our lives, it's also helpful to recall the biblical verse "Do unto others as you would have them do unto you." If you would not enjoy being gossiped about, refrain from gossiping about others. If you would not appreciate having your fashion choices dissected, don't dissect those of others. My stepdaughter came up with the motto "let people live" for someone in her life who she thought had a tendency to get too caught up with what others were doing or not doing. I have found it to be a catchy and useful phrase to call to mind and you might too if you get tempted to go down the gossip path or to be overly concerned with others.

What is important to remember about ahimsa, and about all aspects of the yoga path, is that it is a process and a practice. We don't wake up one day and say "nailed that ahimsa thing, what's next?" Instead, we dedicate ourselves to a path of non-violence, love, and compassion, and do so again and again. Now slip-ups will happen, that is a part of being human, so remember that perfection is neither required nor even sought after.

Do I ever gossip or judge others? Yes, but not often and when I do I get an uncomfortable feeling in my gut that reminds me I'm not acting in line with my values. Then I quickly course-correct and move on. This is what the path asks of each of us. Be mindful of how we show up in the world. Notice where kindness may be lagging and then recommit.

The yama of ahimsa teaches us to respect our connectedness by relating to the world around us with compassion and peace. At the end of every yoga class I've ever attended or taught we recite the Sanskrit word *"Namaste"* in unison. This means the light in me sees and honors that same light that exists in you. It draws us back to the infinity sign—the number eight on its side—that represents our connection and unity. When I feel into the meaning of Namaste, or when I work on bringing more kindness and compassion to my interactions with others and with myself, I can successfully chip away at some of the non-David that surrounds me. I get closer to the version of myself that can shine some light into my world.

As you can see, ahimsa—and indeed all of the yamas and niyamas—are big ideas with many applications. I invite you to consider how you can invite more ahimsa into your life. It is important to remember that this process is absolutely not a one-size-fits-all. It is unique to each of us, just as our DNA is. Thus, my suggestions below are simply that. They may resonate with you, or they may not. But I encourage you to at least consider them and decide for yourself. And if it feels right, then pick one or two or even three things to work on.

Three practices to consider to activate ahimsa in your life include:

- Notice when you get mired in negative self-talk. Create an antidote. Perhaps a simple "I love you" or "I've got this" to yourself. Or something more specific, like "I deserve love" or "I deserve happiness." Write it down on a piece of paper and keep it with you or put it in the notepad app on your smartphone. Then read it to yourself a lot, day after day or as is most helpful.
- Think about a difficult person in your life. Maybe a mere annoyance, maybe a real thorn in your side. Next, close your eyes, picture them, and then consider sending them some good vibes, wishing them happiness and peace. Consider taking this a step further and actually doing something kind for them.
- Perform a random act of kindness on a regular basis. Perhaps make it every Monday that you do something like pick up the Starbucks order for the person in line behind you; compliment a stranger on how nice their shirt or blouse looks on them (but only if it really does); or send a friend you haven't seen in

a while a card, text, or email telling them you are thinking of them.

- *Satya (truthfulness)*

"Tell the truth," we instruct our children. It's probably one of the first moral lessons we learn and impart. As adults, it can be easy to lose our way with this simple guidance. White lies can become a part of our verbal repertoire, as we tell ourselves we are sparing hurting someone's feelings or making our own lives easier. Everyone does this, though for some it can reveal a deeper less healthy pattern such as being a people pleaser.

I'm raising my hand on this one: guilty. By nature I am a people pleaser. I like to be liked. My husband sometimes quotes Woody Allen quoting Groucho Marx: "I wouldn't want to be a member of any club that would have me as a member." See, my husband is an anti-joiner. I'm the opposite. In fact in my teenage years I liked just about any boy that showed an interest in me. You like me and think I'm cute? Great, let's go out! Sad but true.

Thankfully my powers of discernment have grown over the years, but I still have that deeply rooted desire to please and to be liked. I literally cannot count how many times I have said yes to something, like an event or a get-together, that I knew I couldn't or wouldn't follow through on. As you may have guessed, saying yes when I've needed to say no hasn't generally worked out so well. I imagine the same is true for you. I've gotten myself into some awkward situations because of my lack of *satya*. However, I want to add this is a part of the practice I diligently work on.

Another area where we can practice *satya* is in our friendships. One of my closest girlfriends and I have talked about this a lot. She and I have been tight for many years. We joke that we're sisters from other misters. We tell each other literally everything and call each other out on our bulls**t. She has said many times that through our friendship she has learned what it's like to really be honest in a loving way. We've created such a safe space where she can call me up and tell me something I said or did to hurt her feelings and where I can call her up and tell her she's not been present enough with me. Not every friendship can or even should strive for this level of continuous honesty, but for the special ones that matter the most and have the deepest level of trust, it can be extremely strengthening to practice *satya*.

Author and neuroscientist Sam Harris describes this truth succinctly in his book *Lying*:

> "Honesty is a gift we can give to others. It is also a source of power and an engine of simplicity. Knowing that we will attempt to tell the truth, whatever the circumstances, leaves us with little to prepare for. Knowing that we told the truth in the past leaves us with nothing to keep track of. We can simply be ourselves in every moment."

The last sentence of this passage suggests there is more to truth telling than simply avoiding out and out lies. More specifically, it means to be yourself in every moment.

To begin with, we need to know who we are and what we stand for. We need to tell ourselves the truth. In 1999 when I married my first husband, I was pretty good at fooling myself. He and I looked good together. We seemed good together. Everyone thought we were a great couple. My family loved him and his family loved me. So we must be ready to get married, right? Wrong. Had I been more attuned, I would have seen any number of the signs telling me this was not the right path—not for either of us. But I wasn't attuned enough and so thought I knew more than I actually did. I thought I needed this man and he needed me and that was all there was to it.

I also naively thought that once we got married everything would be okay. It's clear to me now that I was pretty actively engaged in lying to myself. Looking back I sometimes angrily tell myself *I should have known better. I was an intelligent twenty-seven-year-old woman.* And then I allow my self-compassion to kick in, nowadays much sooner than before. We all have blind spots, and often are standing right in the middle of them. That's one important reason why engaging in the practice of *satya* to hone our self-truth-telling skills can really improve the quality of our lives.

Have you ever had a little voice in your head that said "no" to something you were doing but you kept on doing it anyway? I can see you nodding. We're all nodding. How do we begin to listen to our inner voice? The answer is straightforward, though not so easy to achieve. Tune in. Listen. Be curious about what is really going on in our minds and in our hearts. And then tell ourselves the truth.

We can also look at our adherence to *satya* in considering whether or how we encourage others to be truthful with us. Do we provide a safe space for our loved ones to speak their truth, even if it's uncomfortable? When they speak, do we let them have their own truth without imposing our own version? Perhaps the most tangible way we can do this is by creating some space between hearing and reacting. We can learn to pause, listen, and let their words really sink in.

There is a concept in yoga that says we are all on a journey of discovering our true nature. This sense of our own personal truth is an evolving one that is more journey than destination. One that can change as we mature and make our way further down our spiritual paths. Once we discern our truth, the challenge then is putting it into action with integrity and alignment. Or stated differently, having our insides match our outsides. For example, perhaps you care deeply about animal welfare and find the industry of factory farming too much to bear. What would you do if, at a friend's house, you were offered a chicken dish that very may well have come from a factory farm? Assuming you're not a vegetarian, would you ask where the chicken is from and how it was raised? Would you question whether doing so would be rude?

I'll posit that in this scenario you feel encouraged to tell your truth, but in as kind of a way as you can. Perhaps something along the lines of "Thank you so much, I really appreciate this. But I've made a solemn promise to myself to no longer eat meat from factory farms. So can I ask where this is from? If it's from a factory farm then I will just enjoy the amazing salad you've prepared and some delicious bread."

Still, what if your friend gets offended, or even angry? Are you willing to risk an uncomfortable reaction and stand by your truth? Maybe you're not there yet, and that's okay. Perhaps by even considering the question you're inching a little closer to first discerning and then standing firmly in your truth. For this scenario a good alternative may also be that before the event you tell your friend about your dietary restrictions.

I have an important person in my life who has dedicated her professional life to helping some of the most vulnerable amongst us—poverty-stricken mothers, some of whom are addicted to drugs, and who rely heavily on the social safety net of the welfare system. A number of her friends recently voted for a political candidate who vowed to end, or at least greatly reduce, welfare benefits for this population. My friend's truth was clear and had been for decades, so she really struggled with her friends' decisions not aligning with her own deeply held convictions. Ultimately she resolved this conflict by practicing *ahimsa*—she told her friends in a loving and respectful way that she needed to step away from the group because of their differences on this issue, which is so central to who she is. This too was a test of *satya*. In my mind, she excelled at the way she handled the situation.

The famous composer Debussy said, "music is the space between the notes." Carrying this forward, I suggest we find the space between the noise in our lives and not simply listen to one expert or another, one celebrity or another, one politician or another. Rather, we consider cultivating some silence and some stillness; finding our truth from the inside out and not the other way around. Your truth might just be what's in your heart when you get quiet and still enough to hear it. This is where the contemplative practices of the yoga path really can come into play.

You may be saying to yourself now, *but what if the truth is scary? Or it really, truly sucks?* Maybe you've been lying to yourself for years and don't even know what the truth is anymore—like saying you're happy in your marriage, when you're not. Or telling yourself your chosen career path is a good one, when it's really not. Or going along with something as being good enough when really it's barely adequate.

Telling ourselves the truth can be hard. It can be painful, even excruciating. But yoga philosophy insists that it's a part of the path of growth. You already know truth is a part of any growth path, yoga-centered or otherwise. You probably also have some inkling too that really showing up fully in your life and in your world requires you coming from a place of authenticity. This doesn't mean you have to know all the answers. Nor does it mean you have to make all the right choices all of the time. But it does mean you have to be honest, starting with yourself. Honest about your strengths and your limitations.

Three practices you can consider to serve up some *satya* in your life include:

- Watch yourself carefully the next time you either tell a "white lie" or are tempted to. Take a few minutes to explore why you lied—were you trying to spare someone's feelings? Were you being a people pleaser? Consider how you could have simply been honest. Question your assumptions; for example, *If I say no to this event, I'll never be invited again and I'll have no friends and I'll die all alone and get eaten by my cats, who clearly are not vegan.* Make a promise to yourself to tell the truth the next time. And then do.

- Ask yourself this question: *what am I willing to die for?* It's a serious question so give it some thought and time. Journal about it. Next, ask yourself: *am I living my life for that someone, thing, or cause?* Say your answer is you would die to keep the earth safe. What are you doing in your daily life to protect the earth? Consider whether you can or are responsible for doing more.

- If being truthful comes easily for you, ask yourself *how does satya interact with ahimsa?* Ahimsa is the first yama for a reason—it's the most important of all of yoga's precepts. So satya, and each of the other ethical guidelines, always bows to ahimsa. I'll give you an example related to this relationship: are you brutally honest in a way that is unkind? (Heck yeah those jeans make your butt look fat!) Consider how you can soften and maintain the integrity of your words with kindness and compassion.

- *Asteya (non-stealing)*

The yamas have expansive definitions. Just as there is more to ahimsa than not committing murder and more to satya than not lying, there is more to asteya than not being an actual thief. Take a moment to consider all the ways we might inadvertently steal from others. When we are late, we might steal time. When we interrupt, we might steal attention. When we constantly complain or talk incessantly about ourselves, we might steal people's energy.

One step toward better understanding asteya is to ask yourself: *when others speak, do I listen?* Like, really listen, fully absorbed in what they are saying and not thinking about how you will respond? The act of actively listening seems to be somewhat of a lost art in our modern world of multitasking. For instance, consider if you're stealing from a conversation by glancing at your smartphone.

I have a confession: I can be a chronic interrupter. Not because I am trying to hog the spotlight, but because I sometimes rush to finish others' sentences in an effort to show that I am really listening and totally get where they are coming from. The problem is that I'm often wrong. But by being more aware of asteya, and by slowing down and watching myself in my interactions with others, I've been able to make progress at simply engaging in the act of listening. This does not always come easily but I am better at it now than I used to be.

I was recently discussing the idea of asteya with a friend who asked an interesting question I hadn't really thought of. What should we do if someone steals from us? There's a T-shirt I've seen that says, "Do no harm but take no shit." That about sums it up. We yogis are not pushovers. We practice ahimsa (non-violence) but we're nobody's fool.

So if someone steals from you and you want to approach it like a yogi, consider this: Confront them. Call them out on their bad behavior. Seek redress. Be honest. But be appropriately respectful too. Thus, no gratuitous name-calling. And of course absolutely no physical violence. Perhaps even consider refraining from venting to everyone and their sister about how this person wronged you.

Another lens through which to view asteya involves the ways in which we might be unwittingly stealing from ourselves. Let me explain. Society can seem to make endless demands on us—to look a certain way, to make a certain amount of money, to define our success according to certain markers. If we get too caught up in any of these societally-imposed standards, we can lose sight of what is true and beautiful to us. This is where asteya meets satya. I strongly suggest you find your truth and then find the courage to stand by it. By bringing your truth to life in an authentic way, you can move closer to your inner David.

The yamas and also the niyamas, as we will soon see, are oftentimes interwoven. Below are three practices to consider that can help you affirm the idea of asteya:

- Notice whether you actively listen when your partner or bestie is talking. Not with a harsh "OMG I'm such a jerk, I'm already thinking of what I want to say next" attitude, but with a gentle self-reminder to be fully engaged in what your peep is saying (remember ahimsa).

- Watch how you take up physical space. Do you dump your belongings haphazardly around you and around those with whom you share space? Be mindful of not acting like you own the place. Whether in a shared bathroom, on an airplane (your elbows jutting into the space of the person sitting next to you), or at the gym or yoga studio.

- Consider whether you are stuck in a habit of conforming to societal expectations at the expense of doing, or even being, what you truly want. Love wearing white after Labor Day? Do it! Who cares what the fashionistas say. Don't think you really ever want to settle down, get hitched and have a family? Forget the "supposed to" and "should" and forge your own path. Live, and wear, your truth.

- *Brahmacharya (non-excess)*

The literal translation of the yama of brahmacharya is sexual abstinence. The ancient yogis viewed sexual energy as extremely powerful. They believed it should be held within in order to boost vitality and deepen spiritual practice. Celibacy shows up in many spiritual traditions for much the same reason. But for modern yogis who tend to be "householders"—a term intended to denote those of us with families rather than monks living in caves—it has been interpreted as non-excess.

Brahmacharya still often is linked with sexuality in that it asks us to bring our yogic ethics into our intimacies. You may have heard the old joke about adding "...in bed" to whatever proverb you find inside your fortune cookie. It definitely makes the reading of the fortunes more interesting, at least as best as I can recall from my college days ("You will soon come into wonderful luck...*in bed*"). This light-heartedness can be applied to the yamas as well: Be more kind and compassionate *in bed*. Tell the truth *in bed*. Don't steal *in bed*. And so forth.

Brahmacharya goes way beyond "between the sheets." It urges moderation in all areas of our lives where we might otherwise drain our energies. If you hit the bar on Saturday night and overindulge in dirty martinis or Jack Daniels or whatever your favorite libation is, you're not likely to be very present and engaged at the tail end of the night, or the next morning. Same thing with overindulgence in a hefty pizza or a big bag of Twizzlers.

While the excess does not need to be from an actual disorder, like my binge eating, to implicate brahmacharya, I remember from my days of binging how I felt the morning after an extreme overindulgence. Aside from the emotional anguish I was in, my body felt positively abysmal. Lethargic, achy, bloated. It sometimes felt like I spent the entire day just willing the hours to hurry by so the binge could finally be in the rearview mirror—that is until the next one. There is no way back then that I moved through the world with energy or a sense of vitality. I couldn't. And that's really the problem with overindulgence. It robs us of our life energy. It might feel good in the moment, but the feeling is sure to be followed by some degree of suffering.

A caveat is in order here. When I speak of excess, I'm not talking about addiction because I can't. That's way beyond my expertise. Yoga is my area of expertise though so I would like to make a clear point: yoga is not a substitute for mental health services. Or for addiction recovery services. It can absolutely be a useful tool in any healing process, but it's not meant to take the place of Western treatment modalities. Yes, yoga helped me heal from my binge eating disorder but only after some significant therapy sessions with a professional psychologist.

However, I do not want to gloss over the healing powers of the practice. I have many yogi friends and have read about countless others who have experienced significant healing through yoga—healing from abusive relationships, sexual assault, debilitating illness or injury, devastating loss, and yes, from addiction. Yoga, if practiced wisely and authentically, supports healing in conjunction with separate primary treatments.

Several years ago I went through a period of spending way too much money on clothes. Shopping, particularly online, became a way of tuning out, getting distracted, and getting sucked into a "if I have such and such, I'll be happy" kind of mindset that often is really a recipe for feeling empty and frazzled.

Fortunately before too much harm had been done, I recognized I was getting stuck in a cycle of craving: shopping, feeling temporarily satisfied after caving in to the craving, and then repeating the whole thing over and over again. So I decided to go for a full year without buying a single item of clothing. I did it, and found that not only was it not that hard, it actually felt great. It was quite refreshing. When I wasn't wasting time thinking about the next need-to-have accessory or other closet accoutrement, I had so much time and energy for, well, life! And while I lifted my self-imposed ban at the end of that year, to this day my shopping has never slipped back to that state of perpetual craving and seeking.

Looking back at my mild "shopping addiction," I can see the wisdom of brahmacharya. What I had was never enough. The itch for a new pair of high-heeled boots was only temporarily scratched after the purchase. But before too long another itch arose. I was stuck in a repetitive loop that impeded my ability to be fully present and engaged with my life. I realize too excess overwhelmed my senses, rendering it literally impossible to be mindful in the moment. I'm reminded of the Dave Matthews song *Too Much*. In it he intones:

> *I'm not satisfied*
> *The hunger keeps on growing*
> *I eat too much*
> *I drink too much*
> *I want too much*
> *Too much*

I can see in these lyrics how a sense of overindulgence is paired with the belief of not having, or not even being, enough. The answer is not to forego all worldly pleasures, including those that are supposedly "bad" for us. Rather, to approach the yama of brahmacharya in a healthy way, it is helpful to think about a balance in life's pleasures.

Brahmacharya does not ask the modern yogi to *never* have sex, to *never* have one more drink, or to *never* have that extra scoop of ice cream. I suggest actually that rigidly restricting your consumption is just as dangerous as engaging in excess. "Always" and "never" are dangerous words on the path of yoga; the key is the middle way.

It's easy to see how our tendency to either overdo it or to overly restrict ourselves is inextricably linked to a deep sense of lacking. Take a moment to simply consider the word "enough" as it applies to you. Do you feel as though you have enough? Make enough? Are enough? For most of us the answer is a resounding no to at least one of these, if not all three. How can we start to shift this sense of needing more—say, to be richer, thinner, prettier, smarter; the list is virtually infinite—to being satisfied with who we are and what we have?

I understand in the few seconds it took for you to read this last sentence you may have already leaned toward deciding the question is not worthy of your attention because you really do need more X or need to be more Y. But first please consider this. I'm not suggesting having goals, whether they be for better finances, fitness, sex, or anything else is bad or somehow not part of the yoga path. Speaking for myself, when I sat down to write this book I had a goal in mind. But I didn't approach the endeavor with a sense that if I didn't finish it, or if it never got published, or if I never sold a single copy, I would not be enough.

This is one example of how I successfully evolved in an area, yet, let me remind you that I'm still and always will be a student; that I struggle with my own stuff as much as the next yogi. Walking the path of yoga has helped me establish a stronger, surer sense of my self. But it's not obviated my insecurities or doubts. Some mornings I wake up and look in the mirror and the first word I hear in my head is "ugly." Some evenings as I lay my head down on my pillow the last word I hear in my head is "asshole" as I recall that I forgot to return a client call or realize that I nagged my husband again. Ten or fifteen years ago I would have stewed in my self-criticism for hours or even days. Now though I notice when my hurtful, anti-ahimsa inner dialogue starts in and I can pretty quickly come back to center.

How then does setting goals fit within the framework of yoga? Yoga teaches us to have goals, but to not be so invested in the results of our efforts that we become unmoored if things don't go as planned. By carrying that much attachment, it is inevitable we will suffer, whether or not the project at hand succeeds as hoped or doesn't. If we don't meet our goals, attachment ensures that we will suffer from disappointment or worse. Ironically, suffering is also inevitable even if we do meet our goals if we come from a place of attachment. Change is inevitable, and clinging too tightly will lead to unhappiness when it comes.

I've been on this earth long enough to know that "I will be happy when [fill in the blank]" is simply a myth. Count how many times you have said that to yourself and then even achieved or attained said happiness-prerequisite, only to soon find that life was still, well, life with ups and downs, excitements, and disappointments. But most likely, before too long you had a new mantra of "I'll be happy when..." I know I've played that game more times than I can count. Friends, it's time for a new way.

The wild popularity of the best-seller *The Life-Changing Magic of Tidying Up,* in which author Marie Kondo makes the case for stripping down our material possessions to live a life of more simplicity and joy, is a nod to brahmacharya's relevance in today's world. Kondo persuasively links discarding what you don't really need to sparking joy in your life. It comes back to the premise that the healthiest path is one of moderation—not too much, not too little.

Three practices for your consideration to bring on some brahmacharya include:

- Ask yourself in what ways do you overindulge. Food, drink, sex, something else? See if just for one week, or even one day if a whole week is too daunting, if you can shed the excess. For instance, maybe cut out sugar for a week and see how you feel. Or take a break from shopping knowing that you have all you really need.

- Schedule a thirty-minute time slot to clean out a drawer, cabinet, or closet. Toss or give away what you don't need. Look at the newly organized space and see how you feel. Remember this feeling and consider scheduling a longer period of time to tackle a larger area of space.

- Notice if you have a "more is more" mindset. See if the next time you go for a walk, run, or yoga class, you can approach the activity with a commitment to finding the middle way. Remember, not too much, not too little. Maybe slowing down or even stopping to look at a really gorgeous tree you usually barely notice on your route. Maybe a few more child's poses on your yoga mat.

- *Aparigraha (non-possessiveness)*

The yama of aparigraha asks us to not hold on too tightly. At its core, aparigraha is really about not clinging. To material things, to people, to experiences, to our physical bodies. One interpretation is "greedlessness"—letting go of the greedy tendencies we possess. Everyone has some degree of greed; of wanting more, of not being satisfied with what we have. A greedy approach to life fits into the paradigm of a zero-sum way of thinking: if I lose, you win; if I win, you lose. When we begin to see the falsity of this, we can better let go of the fear of not having enough and come into a more generous mindset.

Aparigraha does not ask you to renunciate material possessions. It doesn't shame you for seeking or already having prosperity. Rather, it asks you to examine your underlying beliefs about why you want more. Perhaps it's for good reason; say, to support your loved ones. But if you do it to possess status symbols in an effort to gain approval from others, then you are fighting with aparigraha.

A spiritual teacher of mine once said, "If you want to be unhappy, compare, compare, compare." She knew that comparison is a speedy route to feeling dissatisfied with what you have/who you are, and a sure way to get trapped in clinging to what you think you need or want. Yet, you might be thinking that some comparison can be motivating. Like, for instance, seeing the yogi practicing next to you take an interesting variation of a pose. This could motivate you to try something you otherwise would not have even thought about.

I suggest though that this isn't really comparison. Rather, it's finding inspiration from those around us. When practiced in a balanced way, sparking our ingenuity by looking at others can be extremely helpful and even further our growth. We start to get into trouble however when we look at Yogi Yolanda with the practically gravity-defying acts of postural prowess, and then feel inferior. That's the kind of comparison that guarantees malcontent.

My stepdaughter, wise beyond her years, that one, has a favorite quote which also pertains to the idea of comparison: "The only person you should compare yourself to is the person you were yesterday." This speaks to the process of continual upward movement. Not that we can't sometimes take two steps backwards in our journey, but hopefully the overall trajectory of our inner lives is one of growth.

While I love the above quote about only comparing yourself to yourself of yesterday, this approach will surely backfire if we apply it to our physical selves as we age. I'm forty-six and not doing too badly. I eat well, exercise regularly, and generally take good care of myself. But aging is inevitable. My knees are not the knees of a twenty-five-year-old. Or a thirty-five-year-old.

If I cling to the idea that my knees need to be smooth and wrinkle-free, I'll experience some degree of suffering. By even using this example (if you're under forty, odds are that you've never really thought about your knees—ah, the joys of youth!), I've revealed that I can get tripped up when applying aparigraha to my aging body. But there's rich juice here to work with. I can see my clinging and attendant suffering and then work on it. I work on it by seeing it for what it is, attachment, and loosening my grip, maybe even just a minuscule amount to begin with. This too is yoga.

The Buddhists say that everything in this world arises, abides, and then ultimately dissolves. This includes our bodies. For those of us considered "middle aged" or somewhere north of middle age, yoga has so much to teach about acceptance when it comes to our physical selves. Despite our society's seeming obsession with and adoration of youth, and the markedly different way many of us view our own aging, the universal energy that encompasses us all evidently does not intend for us to stay, or look, young forever.

Thus, aparigraha asks us to shift our attitude to accept what is, instead of cling to what was. To find peace with where we are in this moment, rather than worrying ourselves to death over what might be in the next moment. And to understand deep in our bones that with age comes experience, life lessons, and wisdom to help us embrace our aging selves with honor, self-care, and love.

To me, aging gracefully means being, feeling, and even looking my best for wherever I am on my personal journey. I don't want to look or feel like I'm twenty-five. But to look and feel like my best damn forty-six year old self! And I trust I'll be singing the same tune when I'm sixty-six, seventy-six, eighty-six, and so on.

How we treat the earth is another metric of how we are doing vis-à-vis the yama of aparigraha. Do we take more than we need, or more than our fair share? Aparigraha asks us to be mindful in our utilization of natural resources. The "reduce, reuse, recycle" campaign is, in my mind, a nod to aparigraha.

At the risk of sounding a little corny, I believe there is a universal energy of giving and receiving. Aparigraha asks us to feel into a sense of abundance and trust in this universal energy. However, if we live in fear that we won't have or be enough, we can find ourselves in a state of contraction and can even feel this physically as shallowness in the breath, tightness in the shoulders, cramping in the belly. It's as if we are physically battening down the hatches in preparation for a storm, which clearly is not a useful stance if we are looking to receive.

When our fear causes us to hold on to everything we have as if for dear life, we unwittingly shut down the natural flow of energy. But when we trust and lean into the idea of abundance, things tend to flow more smoothly.

This is what aparigraha can teach us. It moves us away from a zero-sum mindset and into a sense that we can have, and be, just what we need and want. And when we do this, we chip away a little more at the non-David encasement that surrounds our best and most authentic selves.

This idea of leaning into abundance instead of contracting into fear does not mean that all of a sudden we're like

Dorothy from *The Wizard of Oz* and just only have to click our heels three times and get to where we want to be. No, yoga is not about magic or miracles. It's far more practical.

I have an extremely close friend whose life as she knew it had crumbled. Her husband had been convicted of securities fraud and went to prison with an exceedingly long sentence, seven to twenty-one years. She had three children to support, no source of income, and lots of people who assumed she was in on the fraud. My friend—a woman I adore like a sister—was struggling to keep herself afloat while also providing a home for her children and keeping food on the table. Previously she had worked as a lawyer but now after nearly fifteen years of being out of the workforce and assuming she'd never work as a lawyer again, she began her job search.

Reentry was neither smooth nor easy. Then she got a break. Or so she thought when she was offered a job clerking for a state court judge. But when the judge found out to whom she had been married, the offer was suddenly revoked. After a lot of pavement pounding and rejections, my friend finally caught a break, this time one that was for real, in getting a post as a staff attorney at a Cleveland law firm. The title of staff attorney though basically denoted her status as we-don't-know-if-you-can-cut-it-so-we'll-see-but-no-promises.

My friend went to work, with no choice but to doubt her doubts and the doubts of her doubters, with rusty legal skills and seemingly the odds stacked against her. She forged ahead though and put her nose to the grindstone. She knew she was smart and a quick study, and in under two years went from staff attorney to partner. When I say such a quick ascension is unheard of, I'm not being hyperbolic.

Now, a couple of years since that auspicious start, she's running a nationally known niche law practice with almost more business than she can handle. She speaks at conferences nationwide and has developed a reputation for being one of the very top-tier experts in her competitive field.

My friend had moments of doubts, fears, insecurities, and tears. I know; I was on the other end of the phone line for many of them. She kept at it though, doing the hard work, day after day. And now she's thriving professionally. Beyond thriving. There was no clicking of heels here; there was grit and determination and sweat. She's a great example of leaning into the flow of life with a determined and capable mind and a passionate heart.

While this story about my friend is an extreme example of suffering almost unimaginable adversity and still overcoming the obstacles placed in her path, I believe we all can relate to being down and having to pick ourselves up. We can relate to wanting to say no but circumstances pushing us to have to say yes. Pulling from ourselves an "I can" when we fear that we can't. Stepping into the flow of life instead of throwing up our hands in despair. This is yoga. This is the yamas and niyamas. This is the eight-limbed path. This is where we can overcome our struggles and shed that which is not serving us and move closer to the beautiful, inimitable truth of who we really are.

Three practices you can consider doing to activate aparigraha in your life include:

- Look for an opportunity to give. Maybe to a charity, either with time or money. Or to a friend or family member down on their luck by taking them out for a nice meal or just dropping by to lend a supportive ear.

- Watch your thoughts that can lead to getting stuck in comparison. Do you really wish you had what so-and-so has? A designer handbag, a nice car, a cute spouse, a perky nose? See if you can tell yourself you're good just as you are with what you have—try it repeatedly so that you start to believe it. Maybe even retire the glamour magazines or stop following the Instagram celebs if these things tend to make you feel lousy about yourself. Here's a true story: I remember when I was young I read fashion magazines and played a game with myself. I'd imagine I could pick one thing per page to have as my own. I engaged in a "I'd be happy if" thing that seemed fun in the moment but always left me feeling empty and lacking. Also a true story: I don't read fashion magazines anymore.
- Create an internal talking point for yourself. Perhaps something like "I am ready to receive" or "clinging creates suffering." Write it out. Stick it on your bathroom mirror. Post it in the notes app on your smartphone. Read it. Start to believe it. And then work on it.

The yamas work on their own and in tandem. It's important to remember ahimsa always comes first, and that everything flows from that place of non-harming and compassion. Then there's satya—speak and live your truth; asteya—don't steal from others or from yourself; bramacharya—take what you need and even want, but don't overdo it; and aparigraha—live with a looser grip on the controls. When we hold the different areas of our lives together with the glue of the yamas, a simplicity can arise where we know we are living in integrity and with authenticity. Still, any step at all towards bringing the yamas to life will help bear fruit.

The French writer Voltaire wisely advised not to let perfection be the enemy of the good. In other words, don't do nothing because you can't do everything; carrying that over to yoga, don't get discouraged that you can't tackle the yamas perfectly and thus gloss over them completely. Remember that baby steps are how we learned how to walk. So I suggest you start small.

CHAPTER TWO
THE NIYAMAS – HONORING
YOURSELF

Your relationship with yourself is really where you set the tone for your entire life. The niyamas are largely concerned with this relationship and are often called "internal restraints," as they pertain to our relationship with ourselves. Like the yamas, there are five:

- *Saucha* (purity)
- *Santosha* (contentment)
- *Tapas* (self-discipline)
- *Svadhyaya* (self-study)
- *Ishvara pranidhana* (surrender)

Whereas we can think of the yamas as "do nots," we can think of the niyamas as "do's."

If the idea of having your very own Michelangelo to carve out your inner David appeals to you, the niyamas get right to the nitty gritty of shedding that which doesn't serve you so that you can bring your best self forth and brightly shine in the world. As with the yamas, it is helpful here also to start small, lest you get overwhelmed. I suggest you read through this chapter and then pick one niyama to get started with.

- *Saucha (purity)*

Saucha, also translated as cleanliness, asks you to take care of your internal and external surroundings by keeping your body neat and clean and well-tended to, and by keeping your home or office neat and clean and well-tended to. When we move from a place of orderliness devoid of clutter, there is a lightness and a sense of freedom that often comes as a result. Have you ever tried to write a paper or work on an important project in an office or at a desk that was in disarray? It's not easy. In fact, it can be so hard that perhaps the hours you should have spent on your project were spent instead on straightening up and cleaning just so you could think straight. When we engage in the practice of saucha, both inside and outside, we thus free up our minds and our bodies to pursue what is really important.

As the nineteenth century French novelist Gustave Flaubert wrote, "be regular and orderly in your life, so that you may be violent and original in your work." He was speaking to the idea captured by the niyama of saucha, which in everyday language means that when we are unencumbered by the weight of physical, mental, and emotional clutter, we can see clearly and imagine expansively.

I recently completed an advanced teacher training program with Rolf Gates, a leader in the yoga world, a teacher, author, teacher of teachers, and all around amazing man. He has dedicated his life to the practices of yoga so that he can live, and show others how to live, with compassion and peace. In his famous book *Meditations from the Mat,* Rolf explores the Yoga Sutras in all of their fullness. Writing on the niyama of saucha he states:

"Our body is the home of our spirit. It is the means by which we enact our beliefs. Therefore, the maintenance of the body is a spiritual duty, an act of love not only toward ourselves but toward all humanity."

Thus, we can consider attending to the body as an important part of our spiritual practice. Like most things on the path of yoga though, there is not a one-size-fits-all answer. Perhaps you practice saucha by drinking more water, by going to the gym or the yoga studio more often, or by eating more leafy green vegetables. One of my favorite yoga teachers once referred to her pedicure as an exercise in saucha since keeping her feet neat and pretty showed self-care and purity. There is no end to how we modern yogis can creatively apply these ancient principles!

Like the lethargy that results from overindulging as we explored earlier with respect to brahmacharya, saucha asks us to lighten our proverbial loads by being orderly and organized. But that alone is not enough to capture the essence of this niyama. We also need to look beyond our physical lives and into our internal state of affairs. If we have a voice in our head that is stuck on self-pity or blame or anger, I suggest we have some internal spring-cleaning to do. After all, we are each the caretakers of our own bodies, minds, and spirits. There is a saying that goes "how you do anything is how you do everything." If you accept this, then if we don't take care of ourselves, we can't possibly take care of those around us.

Perhaps you've heard the quip that hanging onto anger and resentment is like drinking poison. If our minds are cluttered and full of chaos, the most organized outer environment in the world won't deliver us the sense of peace that comes from engaging in true saucha. However, it is important to recognize that an organized outer environment can provide some support for greater internal peace.

There's a lot of talk about forgiveness in most spiritual traditions, including yoga. We don't necessarily, or even typically, forgive to provide absolution to the person who wronged us. Rather, we forgive for ourselves so we can lessen our burden of carrying around a grudge. Engaging in forgiveness in this way is an exercise in saucha. It is also a way of shedding that which is not serving us, that which is clouding the beauty of our authentic selves.

I suggest you try this exercise. Call to mind someone who you believe wronged you at some point. Can you see him or her in your mind's eye? Now really feel into the resentment that you carry around due to whatever it was this person did. Does it serve you? Does it make you feel open and light? If you're being honest with yourself you're probably shaking your head.

Now imagine this resentment leaving your body, mind, and heart; disappearing into the ether. What does this feel like? This is not a rhetorical question. Give yourself a few moments to consider. Or, perhaps you'd like to hang on to the resentment—and I'm not being snarky here, maybe you really are not ready to let it go yet. That's okay. Or maybe you're ready to let go just a little. That's also okay. Consider this a sincere invitation to open the door, however wide you wish—not for the sake of the wrongdoer, but for yourself. Know too that you may be bestowing some psychic benefit to the one who caused you harm, such as demonstrating a generosity of spirit.

One of the most important fruits of any spiritual practice is living with authenticity. Or expressed in another way, meaning what you say and saying what you mean; having your insides match your outsides. This is where the yama of satya teams up with the niyama of saucha.

Because the opposite, the hypocrisy of not living in alignment, can get you in trouble. Take for example some of our most infamous public figures. Remember Ted Haggard? He was the leader of an evangelical Colorado megachurch who was extremely vocal and influential in arguing against gay rights. As it turned out Haggard, married with children, had been in a three-year homosexual relationship. Needless to say, his professional and personal life suffered immensely, not to mention the hurt and embarrassment his hypocrisy caused his family.

Another aspect of saucha that we can explore is the finding of purity by simply engaging with the present moment. In part this can be experienced by removing clutter that inevitably results when we try to do too many things at once. A Zen master once answered the question "What is Zen?" by saying, "Doing one thing at a time." For those buying in to the societal message that doing as many things possible at the same time means you are more accomplished and productive, you may want to reconsider this. If you're on a phone call and also scrolling through Facebook, you're not really present in either activity. I have to admit I have done this before. I've also been on work calls while online shopping for my next great pair of high-heeled sandals.

We can get all down on ourselves about our imperfections. But what I try to do and suggest you consider doing the same, is instead remember that this thing called yoga is a journey more than a destination. It's about being engaged in the work, not nailing it every time. As awareness expands, we can make better choices more often.

Three practices you may want to try to invoke saucha in your life include:

- Notice your tendency to multi-task. Then take an entire day and commit to doing one thing at a time. If that's too daunting, how about doing it for an hour? Or pick a modest amount of time, say five or ten minutes, and just sit and do nothing except notice your breath. In other words, meditate.
- Pick an area of your home or workspace to organize. For an entire week, keep that area neat and tidy. Maybe this simply means making your bed each morning instead of telling yourself that before too long you'll be back in it so why bother.
- Pick one way you can engage in a purity-cultivating act of self-care. Perhaps switching out your usual laundry detergent for one that's organic and chemical-free. Or, if you live on coffee or otherwise ignore your body's need to hydrate, commit to getting in eight glasses of water a day. You can be creative here and not limit yourself to just the outside. Perhaps for an internal kind of cleaning out, maybe for a day or two lay off of that snarky voice in your head that is overly critical of others.

- *Santosha (contentment)*

Santosha is all about cultivating a sense of being content with your lot in life, enjoying the process of your path unfolding, and not simply hopping from one attainment or goal to the next. Yoga philosophy teaches that the primary causes of suffering are attachment—holding on too tightly to things we want—and aversion—pushing away too forcefully things we don't want. The niyama of santosha suggests a middle way: letting go of wanting and not wanting and instead being okay with what is.

Please consider doing this exercise. Imagine for a moment what it would be like to want for nothing. To neither cling to that which is pleasing nor to push away that which is not. How many of your days are filled with the story of wanting and not wanting? Whether material goods, physical accomplishments, professional or educational accolades, a glass of wine—we want these things, and badly. While infirmity, setbacks, and failures—we really, really don't want these things. Yes this is just the nature of being human, and yet there is a way beyond the suffering that necessarily attends our wanting and not wanting.

Step back a moment to explore just how antithetical to contentment it is to want things to be a certain way, and only that way. Consider Oscar Wilde's words in *Lady Windermere's Fan*:

> "In this world there are only two tragedies. One is not getting what one wants, and the other is getting it."

Huh? Why is getting what you want a tragedy?

In a word, "impermanence." Nothing lasts forever; everything changes. The Greek philosopher Heraclites captured this inescapable truth when he wrote:

> "No man ever steps into the same river twice, for it's not the same river and he's not the same man."

As just one example of this, the lining of your stomach is renewed every few days, immersed as it is in digestive acid. Your epidermis, the outer layer of skin, is completely replaced across your entire body with a brand new layer about every six weeks. Put that in the weird but true file. Given that change is an inevitable part of the universe, it follows that getting what you want can lead to suffering when you become attached to your prize and want it to stay just as it is. But, it can't; that's simply not how life works. As the Buddhists know, everything in this world arises, abides, and then dissolves.

How then do we find the healthy way of santosha? A simple shift from looking outward to looking inward is one way to start. Rolf Gates talks about the process of interiorization: looking within yourself to find fulfillment, instead of seeking it elsewhere which is how many of us get through life.

I remember so clearly the very early days of my immersion in all things yoga. I wanted to know what yoga had to say about this, and about that, and about the other thing. I asked my teachers a lot of questions.

Then one day I was exercising at a local gym and I overheard this woman on the machine behind me talking— she was gossiping about me to her friend! Let's just say she wasn't spewing compliments. In fact, her comments were downright catty and mean. The next day I cornered my yoga teacher after class and insisted on knowing what yoga had to say about what happened in the gym. *Should I have confronted Mrs. McNasty at the time? Called her out? Ignore the whole thing?* My teacher looked at me right in the eye and calmly said, "It is not your business what anyone thinks of you." *Come again?* She must have seen the confusion on my face because she simply and slowly repeated herself.

I thought about her words often in the coming hours, days, and even years. What a revolutionary concept and one that was hard for me to wrap my head around. Remember, I really like to be liked. Even today though I still struggle with wanting to be liked and seeking external approval. I may always struggle with this to some degree. But I'll tell you something—with the help of that wisdom "It is not your business what anyone thinks of you"—I care less now than I did when I was younger. The point is that it is incredibly healthy and santosha-building to look for your happiness and satisfaction from within, not from without.

Which leads me to another story I think you'll enjoy. A few months ago I slept through my six am yoga class—that's every teacher's nightmare. Thankfully one of my fellow teachers had risen early to get her own practice in so she taught the class for me. But I was mortified and spent most of the day kicking myself and sending to my boss texts with remorse and apologies. He owns a yoga studio, not a downtown law firm, so naturally I texted: "you still love me, right?" Not missing a beat, he texted back: "stop seeking approval." I laughed out loud. He got it, and me, and sent me back inside on my own journey.

Hearing someone trash-talk you behind your back or sleeping through your alarm, unpleasant as those may be, are not earth-shattering events. How do you gain that perspective when your mind is screaming? How do you go inward and not worry about what others are saying, thinking, and judging when the stakes are even higher? When they involve your children or your livelihood or the well-being of a loved one?

It is not easy, to be sure. But this is where the practice can take us. And this is why, ideally, we still maintain our engagement in the practice when things are going relatively well. Because it is then when we can start to really grow our roots and become a steady, unflappable tree. If we wait until the storm hits to start applying the principles of the yamas and niyamas, and indeed all aspects of the yoga path, we likely will be overwhelmed and underprepared.

There's a paradox in learning not to seek or strive, but rather to accept what is. When we come from a place of acceptance of where we are in any given moment, the growth we seek can more readily come within reach. I know this to be true with respect to my recovery from my binge eating disorder. It was only when I could accept the moment I was in—far from where I wanted to be—that I could begin to heal and move past my own suffering. By loosening my grip and not trying to force change, I inched closer and closer toward my own recovery. Santosha helped light the way.

Lest you think you can nail santosha by leaning back in your recliner with a glass of Pinot Grigio, throwing up your free hand and declaring "it is what it is," giving up all effort and goals in life, don't get too comfortable. This is not *c'est la vie* about striving or having goals. You can engage, and I encourage you to do so often, in efforts towards your well-thought out goals.

The question is really about whether you can soften yourself up a little bit. Accept where you are right now, even in the midst of the working and striving, and keep going with a modicum of contentment in the place where you find yourself. This may seem like a blurry line: strive, but not too much; accept, but don't be complacent. However, I encourage you to lean into this idea, let it simmer, and see what unfolds.

That's what I learned first-hand from a regular yoga student at Yoga Roots, the studio where I teach. Rachel practiced every weekday morning, like clockwork. Not only was she there and ready to practice, she was almost always there by bike. Did I mention I live in Cleveland? Sometimes, the weather really sucks here. But if at all possible, Rachel came on her bike.

RADI8

A few weeks ago Rachel and I were taking the same class. About halfway through, for no apparent reason, she fell out of her down-dog and onto her mat. We naturally stopped to see if she was okay; she said she was fine. With one little caveat. She could not move her left leg. Somehow in an instant she had gone from flowing through the asana practice to seeming paralysis in one leg.

It turned out Rachel had suffered a stroke. It hit the part of her brain that controls her left leg. Days went by with Rachel in the hospital, paralyzed and with no certainty about whether or not, and if so, how long before she would begin to recover.

Then she started to engage in intense physical therapy to literally retrain her brain to work with her left side. There were no assurances or guarantees. Nonetheless, Rachel did not give in to despair. Truly, she did not. She was at peace and even content. It's hard to imagine how until she revealed her secret: her reservoir of santosha was deep—deep enough to withstand the uncertainty of her prognosis. Three weeks after her stroke, Rachel came home. A couple of days after that she returned to Yoga Roots.

Rachel's mobility was still quite limited so her first day she just lay on her mat. The second day she moved a little. Then she took my class on her third day back and was able to do so much I could barely believe it. She had a brace on her ankle and foot and heart monitors on her chest, but goddamn it she was on her mat! Rachel's recovery has exceeded anyone's expectations.

Every day she gets physically stronger. But what resonates with me most is what happened internally for her. She did not become unmoored, though the logistics of her daily life most certainly did. She remained a rooted tree, content with her lot even as she moved forward. Rachel is putting

53

one foot in front of the other, literally, with a shining spirit and an open heart. To me, she is radiance defined. She embodies her inner David.

Three practices you may want to consider to strengthen your santosha include:

- Tap into a sense of gratitude every day. I often remind my students in the middle of a hard, sweaty practice to take a moment to delight in the fact that they get to be in their bodies with their breath. It's a privilege when you stop and think about it. So I encourage you too to stop and think about it.
- Find a few quiet moments to really reflect on what it would be like to not want what you don't have and to want what you do have. Really imagine this. That sense of peace is yours for the taking if you just slow down long enough to consider it.
- A friend of mine recently saw Sheryl Sandburg of *Lean In* fame speak publicly. She shared that every night before she goes to bed she writes down three things that brought her joy that day. It could be the perfect foam on her latte or a job well done at work. The key is that by knowing she will be engaging in this writing activity in the evening, she actually goes through her days looking for moments of joy. Her brain thus becomes primed and even habituated to look for the good. This variation on the gratitude exercise can be really powerful.

- *Tapas (self-discipline)*

The word tapas derives from the Sanskrit word "tap" which means "to burn." Tapas thus evokes a sense of stepping into the fire of the work we need to do for our own growth. Ancient yogis worked on purifying the body and mind through austerities (think skinny dude with no material possessions meditating in a cave all day). For the modern yogi though there are countless ways to apply tapas such as cultivating dietary discipline. Or making it to your yoga mat more often. Or bringing some drive and elbow grease to a thorny problem at work.

However, here's a cautionary note: engaging in tapas is not about showing off or bragging about the fancy arm balancing pose you just nailed, or how many days you've been on a juice cleanse. The latter may instead be a sign of an eating disorder disguised as spiritual growth. Again, we must bring viveka into play to ascertain what truly serves our growth and what may simply be serving our ego or neuroticism.

On December 31, 2015 I decided to meditate daily in 2016. I had always been drawn to the idea of meditation and had spent a fair amount of time reading about it and talking about it, and had even sat on my meditation cushion practicing meditation from time to time. But I had not yet fully committed to a daily meditation practice. Sensing that was the next frontier in my yoga journey, I set 2016 as the year to make it happen. And I did. Some days I meditated for ten minutes, some days for thirty, some for only five. But the experience was one of tapas. Of cultivating the self-discipline to do something for my own growth. I got my butt to my cushion, every damn day.

There were days and even weeks when I was unsure about the impact my practice was having. My inner voice wondered more than once *why am I just sitting here when I could actually be accomplishing something?* I remember one morning, just a few weeks into the new year with my daily practice, a student who has now become a friend looked at me after I had taught a yoga class and said, "You're different." I had not seen any change in myself. But she saw that I was more grounded and present. She knew about my New Year's resolution and had no doubt it was cultivating growth.

It is not always easy to see how or even whether we are evolving. Sometimes those around us can sense this more clearly. The niyama of tapas asks us to trust in the process of the work we commit to do. As yoga master K. Pattabhi Jois famously said, "Practice and all is coming." My 365-day exercise in tapas did what it was intended to. With my fiery commitment, I had burned up all of the excuses that stood between me and my meditation practice. And in doing so, I got closer to myself; a lot closer. I saw myself and my reactions to various situations more clearly. I cultivated more space so that I could choose how to respond: often with more deliberation and kindness. I grew closer to the version of myself I wanted to be, my David.

Rolf Gates has been quite vocal about his transformation from a man with angry and perhaps even violent tendencies to a peaceful warrior committed to a life of ahimsa and spiritual awakening. He grew up in Boston in the 1970's during the tumultuous time of desegregation and forced bussing. Rolf himself was subject to horrific racism. He now talks with great wisdom about moving past his struggles with race.

In one of our discussions during the course of my teacher training, I asked him how exactly did he get past this particular struggle. I mean, racism still exists, and for many it is a very difficult time to be African American in this country. I'll never forget what he told me. "I can't hate a racist the way I used to." He added: "Once you're a pickle, you can't go back to being a cucumber." Through his yoga practice, Rolf changed. He transformed into a person who is far less able to carry hate or resentment in his heart. That's the power of tapas.

I can just hear my activist teenage daughter reading this and asking, "But shouldn't we hate the racists and do everything in our power to shut them down?" No and yes. Hate is not a vehicle for good. Period. In the words of Mahatma Gandhi, "'Hate the sin and not the sinner' is a precept which, though easy to understand, is rarely practiced, and that is why the poison of hatred spreads in the world." I suggest this means we are at our best when we constructively work for justice and equality, just as many dedicate their lives to doing. (I won't be the least bit surprised, and will be immensely proud, if my daughter is one of them.) The important distinction here is that simply cultivating negativity, judgment, and hate has never solved any of the worlds' problems. To the contrary, it perpetuates a cycle of conflict and violence.

Just Mercy is a New York Times bestseller about the work of the Equal Justice Initiative, a non-profit that provides legal representation to people who have been illegally convicted, unfairly sentenced, or abused in prison. In the book, author and EJI Founder and Executive Director Bryan Stevenson chronicles dozens of cases of overt racism and extreme injustice along with his legal battles to right these heartbreaking wrongs—for example, black men with lower income levels being placed on death row for crimes when there is an abundance of evidence that they are innocent. The disproportionately high rate of black men incarcerated relative to the population as a whole speaks volumes as well.

Stevenson has been likened to a modern-day Atticus Finch, the revered protagonist in *To Kill a Mockingbird*. He has won national acclaim for his work challenging bias in the criminal justice system. If you haven't read *Just Mercy* and care about social justice, run, don't walk, to your favorite bookstore.

I had the privilege of hearing Stevenson talk about his work to a sold-out crowd in Cleveland a couple of years ago. He is funny and self-deprecating while at the same time deep and inspiring. Despite the atrocities he has seen up close and personal, he is not a man filled with hate or rage. Rather, he is a shining example of tapas. He works hard, very hard, in his pursuit of equality in the justice system, and does so with compassion and an open heart.

Tapas is not about finding your inner Sisyphus, the Greek mythological figure who was fated to ceaselessly push a heavy boulder up a mountain only to have it roll back down, and then ceaselessly push it up again, only to have it roll back down every damn time.

The story of Sisyphus also brings to mind a Turkish proverb that goes like this: "No matter how far you have gone down a wrong road, turn back." This refers to a moment in time when we are called upon to discern for ourselves our truest path. If you're on the wrong road, neither yoga nor tapas asks you to muscle through it. To the contrary, the right thing to do is always to turn around. Have you ever embarked on a path that, a few steps in, or maybe a few thousand steps in, you knew was a mistake? But it was hard, inconvenient, or awkward to turn around so you kept going?

I did this with my first marriage. We dated for a few years, lived together for a couple more, all the while I was feeling something wasn't quite right; and yet marriage seemed like the next logical step. So down the same wrong road we continued. If either my ex or I had really stopped to assess, discern, or listen to our hearts, we would have turned back. We would have saved ourselves and our loved ones the heartache of divorce just a couple of years later. But you know how it is—seems like the right thing to do, or it's just too hard or messy to extricate yourself, so you keep going. Tapas says no. Slow down. Get quiet and discern. Then, when you really know you're on the right path, go for it, with everything you've got.

When we engage in tapas we may also find that we shed some unneeded things in our lives. Extra pounds, unhealthy habits, perhaps even some unhealthy people in our lives. I used to not have this kind of discernment about friends. *You like me and think I'm cool? Let's hang out!* As I've gotten farther along on my spiritual journey I have found I have less and less of an interest in small talk. I am much better at resisting the seductive pull of gossip, and I avoid those who engage in it. I'm pickier, more selective about how I spend my time and with whom. There are only so many hours in the day and how we choose to spend them is critically important to who we are and where we are going.

Three practices you may want to consider as ways to tap into tapas include:

- Make a 30-day commitment to something: to meditate, walk, give up sugar, make your bed every day, or whatever you choose that is at least moderately challenging. Then do it for those thirty days.
- The next time you're in a yoga class, see if you can stay in a challenging pose for three breaths longer than you usually do. Even if everyone else has moved on to another pose, stay and breathe. If a yoga class is not how you roll, run, walk or bike for five minutes longer than you set out to and bring some extra discipline and heat as well to your endeavor.

- You can also apply tapas by exercising your willpower. Maybe the next time you're out having cocktails stop after just one glass of wine. Or after a long day at work, just have one little square of dark chocolate. Or maybe abstain all together. Stand in the fire of your discomfort. Breathe through it.

- *Svadhyaya (self-study)*

Yoga philosophy teaches that each of us has a spark of the divine within ourselves. Now before you get too caught up in what the "divine" means or even whether there is such a thing, hang on. We are all part of this thing called life and the experience of being human. If nothing else, beyond differing cultures, ideologies, fortunes and misfortunes, we have that in common.

Svadyhaha asks us to recognize this kernel of goodness/divineness/universalness that we each have. As Patanjali wrote in sutra 2.44 in the *Yoga Sutras*, "Study thy self, discover the divine." You can consider this as getting to know your inner David. Traditionally, yogis engaged in svadhyaya by reading and studying spiritual texts and in that way discerned the truth of the incisive quote by the thirteenth century poet Rumi: "You are not a drop in the ocean; you are the entire ocean in a drop."

Modern yogis can tap into this sense of connectivity by cultivating a warm curiosity towards ourselves and those around us. If we open our hearts and our minds enough, we just might come to realize that we are all part of something bigger than our own individual perspectives can imagine. Again, if you're skeptical, if you're shaking your head or shrugging your shoulders, please don't skip ahead just yet because there's another part of svadhyaya that transcends any kind of spiritual belief.

You can think of the entire practice of yoga as a mechanism to cultivate the capacity to make wise choices in your life. To respond, instead of to react, as meditation teachers often say. How many of your daily choices are simply reactions as opposed to reflections? You grab that second cup of coffee, or slice of bread, or piece of pizza, or glass of wine because you think you need it. Or because you really, really want it. But with greater understanding, we can be less enslaved to our tendencies and go-to reactions than we may think possible now. We cannot break our enslavements, or even notice them for that matter, without svadhyaya. Self-study is a necessary ingredient—perhaps the most necessary—in any growth-oriented dish.

Svadhyaya asks us to see all parts of ourselves with clarity and honesty. It entails shining the light of compassion inward, recognizing that denial and shame thrive in the darkness. Maybe you know this to be true. I do; during my most difficult days of being stuck in my eating disorder I was terribly ashamed. I told no one about it for a very long time. I couldn't—I thought it was proof positive that I was messed up beyond repair or redemption. Now, so many years and a lot of yoga later, I can discuss it and write about it with more grace. It's when we can see clearly and compassionately that our "secrets" begin to loosen their grip on us.

Yoga teacher and author Cyndi Lee describes yoga as not just a work-out, but also as a "work-in." We get quiet, we look inside, and we get to work—perhaps as if culling the weeds from our emotional landscape. So many of us walk around with psychic wounds stemming from childhood difficulties, traumas, disappointments, heartaches, and more. Yet, the niyama of svadhyaya suggests that we can't move onward and upward without seeing and really feeling our hurts. Not with a self-pitying way that keeps us stuck in the past, but with a gentle and honest eye about where we've come from and what we've endured. By seeing with clarity our past and present hurts and the scars that remain, we can begin to heal and then follow the path forward.

When I was in law school I would study for hours at a time in a quiet corner of the library surrounded by books, highlighters, pens, and legal pads. I was rolling up my proverbial sleeves and digging deep. The niyama of svadhyaya is like this: we take our work seriously but instead of just understanding the complexities of, say, civil procedure, we actually strive to gain understanding of the complexities of ourselves.

This doesn't mean we need to lock ourselves away in front of a computer and toil for hours. Because we might also engage in self-awareness as we move through our local Whole Foods—we may find ourselves annoyed with the slowpoke in front of us who is in the way of our reaching for the box of gluten-free pasta. Seeing our annoyance we might notice we have the silly notion that things should be as *we* want them to be, and everyone else be damned. Noticing that, we might laugh a little at ourselves good-naturedly, and then settle into a more patient and compassionate stance with those around us. Or maybe not; or not yet—we might still act out our annoyance feeling we really need that gluten-free pasta right now! When we can begin to see ourselves and our reactions with more clarity, from that place of being truly awake and aware, we can then choose how we move through our world.

What if you can't stand what you see when you get still enough to peer underneath the hood? This is where you are asked to marry ahimsa with svadhyaya; to be kind to yourself.

Catch yourself as you hurl unkind words at yourself and hold yourself a little more gently. Yes this can be quite difficult. Yet, before you write it off as something you cannot do, give it a try. It may feel awkward or inauthentic at first. But don't give up quite yet. Staying with the discomfort may be the most significant thing you can do for your own growth.

Another aspect of svadhyaya involves seeing ways in which we behave that are driven by our ego. The ego is an I-focused way of moving through the world. Like a toddler who only sees things through the lens of her own perspective, our egos walk around only concerned with how things in our days impact us and no one else.

I had a friend in law school who asked one time how I did on the constitutional law exam at the end of our first year. So I told him and he became visibly upset that I had apparently gotten a better score than he had. "Great," he lamented, revealing the intensely competitive environment that characterized law school. "Now I've got to go spend more money on my therapist." His response was tongue-in-cheek and mildly funny, yet it also felt true. My good score made him feel badly about himself. That was his ego talking. If he was able to engage in self-study in that moment, he might have been able to see that his ego-centered mindset, his feelings of insecurity, were quite unhelpful to his well-being.

When we compare ourselves to others, we breed discontent. We also miss out on the opportunity to practice *mudita*, translated from Sanskrit as sympathetic or unselfish joy. There is a sense of purity and well-being when we can delight in the fortunes of our loved ones, friends, and even those we don't know. As my powers of discernment have grown, I look for friends who cheer me on when I experience success. And I love it too when my besties nail something they've worked on.

The opposite of mudita is schadenfreude, a German word describing the sense of pleasure or joy one gets from the downfall or misfortune of another. Have you ever had a friend who seemed begrudgingly happy when you did well, but was almost overly sympathetic and seemed to derive some pleasure when things did not go your way? Me too. With friends like those, who needs enemies? We should all be so lucky to have people in our life who practice mudita with us, and to whom we return the favor.

Three practices you might consider to help you simmer in svadhyaya include:

- Journal. Not just about your hopes and dreams or disappointments, but about how you react to getting or not getting what you want. Do you get all fired up? Do you sink into sadness? Journal about your mental chatter, your go-to patterns. Get to know yourself; as they say on Instagram: #nofilter.
- Practice svadhyaya on your yoga mat. What gets you into reactivity? A hard pose? A not-hard-enough pose? Does your mind wander a lot and if so where does it go? If you're sans yoga mat, try this technique of simply witnessing yourself as you go through your day—if the car in front of you is too slow, how do you react?
- Meditate. The quickest way to get to know what's going on behind the curtain is through meditation. Much more on this in the coming chapters.

- *Ishvara pranidhana (surrender)*

The final niyama of ishvara pranidhana translates as surrender to God. Again we are confronted with the topic of the "divine." I definitely get tripped up by the "G" word; maybe you do as well. So you might be wondering if yoga is a religion. Or whether you have to believe in God to be a yogi. While some may disagree, my answer is a resounding no to both questions.

Yoga is an inclusive path—all religions welcome; atheists and agnostics too. It is a spiritual path to be sure, but it can just as easily co-exist with religion or lack thereof. It is a living philosophy. In describing this niyama in her fabulous book *Do Your Om Thing*, yoga teacher and author Rebecca Pacheco writes:

"When the final niyama, ishvara pranidhana, asks us to surrender to God, it's not choosy about who or what God is. It reminds us that a higher power exists, and yoga can unite us with that higher power; however, your higher power can just as easily be a bearded man or part-elephant deity, or the transcendent feeling of watching a sunset or holding a newborn."

Furthering Pacheco's analysis, ishvara pranidhana simply asks us to surrender. Period.

To what?

Maybe just to the inescapable fact that we cannot control everything in our lives. If you have kids, you know this to be undeniably true. You want your kid to do X—eat some veggies, clean her room, practice her musical instrument, call her grandmother. But she does Y. You cannot control this all. The same applies to grown ups—spouses, significant others, friends. At some point, and I recommend sooner rather than later, you must surrender. If you don't, you'll be banging your head against the wall until the cows come home.

By surrender I do not mean throwing your hands up in the air and ceasing to care. Or stopping to put forth any effort. Surrender is about swimming with the current, not against it. It's important that I emphasize you still need to swim. You've probably heard about athletes tapping into this state of "flow," as it is often called, or being "in the zone."

If you're from Cleveland as I am, or have any interest in basketball whatsoever, you've seen the greatest basketball player in the world, LeBron James, play. It's a thing of beauty to behold. No matter what is going on around him, James appears to be in a state of total presence and connection to what is transpiring. He surrenders to the moment before him and because of this, his herculean feats on the court appear almost effortless.

Clearly, there is also plenty of brilliant talent and a strong work ethic associated with his athleticism. With countless hours of hard work under his belt, he is able to be unfailingly present and engaged in each moment as it arises, and then in the one after that, and in the one after that. James provides a powerful example of the interplay of working hard and honing one's craft, with surrendering to what flows as a result.

We too can find the peace of surrender when we put forth our best effort and then release control of the result. This is one of the primary lessons in the *Bhagavad Gita*, perhaps the best-known writing on yoga philosophy after the *Yoga Sutras*.

The *Gita* is a Hindu scripture that tells a two thousand-year-old story—essentially about how to live a fulfilling life—through a dialogue between the protagonist, a warrior named Arjuna, and his divine mentor Krishna. Krishna counsels the young Arjuna to "perform the necessary action" but to act "without concern for results." He further advises that the way for Arjuna to accomplish his highest purpose is by "surrendering all attachments."

Thus, yoga philosophy teaches us to put forth effort into our life's work, and then to surrender the fruits of our actions, recognizing those are not ultimately up to us. The niyama of ishvara pranidhana speaks to this in a succinct way.

Three practices you may consider to ignite ishvara pranidhana include:

- Set an intention. I often ask yoga students to do this at the beginning of the practice; and when I practice I often set my own. One of my go-to intentions is to simply be present, aware of each moment as it unfolds, and to notice that if my mind wanders off to simply come back to my breath and the sensations arising in my body. You can set an intention for your day, or your month, or your life. Then, having set a clear intention for yourself, release it to the universe or to whatever higher power you believe in. See if you can cultivate a sense of trust that things will unfold just as they are meant to.
- Notice an area in your life where you can be a little less controlling. Then, be a little less controlling. Maybe loosen up on the losing battle of how clean you want your home be. Or make a commitment to go easy on nagging your spouse for a week. Give yourself time to think of something that could make a difference not just for you, but for your loved ones.
- Do something because you love to do it, and forget about the desired result. As I wrote this book, I spent hours and hours lost in the pleasure of putting pen to paper and really enjoyed the process. But I also spent a fair amount of time worrying about the outcome.

What if it sucks? What if no one wants to read it? What if every publisher I send it to laughs out loud at how crappy it is? Through looking inward though, I relearned to recognize that yoga asks me to put forth the effort and to let go of the result. Knowing this and trying to live this, I was able to enjoy the writing process much more than I would have otherwise.

CHAPTER THREE
ASANA – MOVING YOUR BODY
TO TAP INTO YOUR VITALITY

Research on the physical and psychological benefits of exercise confirms the catchy motto you may have heard, "movement is medicine." It's true. The asana practice is an amazing form of physical exercise that can build strength, flexibility, balance, and stamina, and basically keep your entire body looking and feeling supple.

This is not an exercise book, nor a book on the technical aspects of the asana practice. If you're looking for those, they abound. Baron Baptiste's *Journey Into Power* is a great one to start with. I used it often when I started creating a home yoga practice. I also recommend Cyndi Lee's *Yoga Body, Buddha Mind*. What I'm interested in sharing is that having a movement practice generally, and an asana practice specifically, can help us find that inner spark we know when we see it in others. That *je ne sais quoi*: "I've got something goin' on ... I take care of myself ... I value my vitality and my health."

This ineffable quality is not dependent on how much we weigh or what size our waist is. It really isn't. There's a pithy internet meme going around that asks, "How do you get a bikini body? Put a bikini on your body." I love that! It's the truth and it speaks to my point.

Asana and movement as part of the yoga path are about creating health and radiance from the inside out, not trying to fit your outsides into some societally imposed vision of what looks good. It's about learning to feel good in your body; whether you're a woman at a size 6 or a size 16, or a man size medium or a size XXXL. It's about treating your body as the home of your spirit. So having a regular movement practice is a critical step in the right direction.

The yoga movement that I envision is a big-tent party. Everyone is invited. No tryouts necessary; everyone's made the team. I am involved as a volunteer with the Cleveland Rape Crisis Center, a national leader in sexual assault response and prevention. Every year the center holds a day for girls' empowerment, bringing resources and body-positive events to a large group of adolescents from at-risk environments. The day includes such activities as yoga, self-defense, dance, and also provides the participants with education and resources to foster self-care and the development of practical life skills. Naturally, I teach parts of the yoga. It's a come-as-you-are-no-experience-necessary endeavor. The girls get a taste of moving in time with their breath and exploring how that feels in a safe, judgment-free environment. There's a lot of giggling, to be sure. However, the goal is for the girls to walk out feeling good about being in their bodies. It's a healthy example of the inclusivity of the practice.

Rolf Gates teaches that the posture is simply the position the body is in at a given moment; the yoga is *how* you are being in that particular posture. This sentiment captures an important point about the practice—finding the yoga in the moment, whether in a physical, emotional, or spiritual way.

I am reminded of a conversation I once had with my husband before we were married. He asked me to take care of myself in some way; I honestly can't remember the details but that wasn't the significant part of the exchange.

I replied "I'll try."

"Don't try," he said. "Be a tree."

I looked at him questioningly and then he told me to stand up straight. "Now, *try* to be a tree."

I stood there just staring back at him.

"Go on, try."

I pressed my feet into the floor and straightened my spine a little.

"Okay, now *be* a tree."

I breathed in deeply, firmly rooted both feet to the ground, and lifted the crown of my head high. I immediately felt taller (sadly for my 5'1" frame this sense was metaphysical, not literal), straighter, more grounded. I got the point.

Don't simply *try* to do something. Find the qualities within yourself that will enable you to actually do it. The difference is not just semantic. It's intentional. In the story I just described, I felt the difference from my head to my toes. And although this exchange preceded the beginning of my lifelong love affair with yoga by at least a year, it has yoga written all over it. And it captured Rolf's point that yoga is about *how* you show up in any given moment, not about what you happen to be doing.

The asana practice—particularly when we find the synchronicity of breath and movement—is an amazing place to feel into this idea of stepping into each moment with presence and mindfulness. Standing tall and sweeping our arms over our heads, for example, we take in a deep, nourishing breath; then swan-diving our arms down by our sides and all the way to the ground to fold forward, we let out all of the air.

Something magical happens when we combine our movements and our breath. We shift from a place of thinking to a place of feeling. And as we nourish every nook and cranny of our body with our breath, we find a sense of vitality, as if we are coming alive.

I've continued to apply the singularly-focused effort my husband was talking about—to *be* a tree—throughout my life. But let me backtrack for a moment. Several months after he and I had that conversation, our relationship crumbled. I was heart- broken, and pregnant with our daughter. I knew I had to act out of strength, not just for myself but for our child too. So I got a job with a big law firm hundreds of miles away from him, but closer to my family, packed up and set off to create a new life as a single mother.

I was *being* a tree—applying focus and resolve to a difficult situation; staying strong and forward-looking. What I really wanted to do was lay down and cry. To be honest, I did some of that too. While our story has become a happy one (we reunited right after our daughter was born), I had no expectation that it would when I left.

Again, harkening back to Rolf's wise words, the posture of my life was what was happening—I was pregnant and single and I needed to build a home in which to raise my girl. The yoga I mustered was found in my own strength to be that tree. To move, to work hard and establish myself professionally in a new city, and to be emotionally, physically, spiritually, intellectually, and mindfully prepared to go it alone.

This "*be* the tree" exercise also translates beautifully to the asana practice or really any form of intentional movement. I can be in a Warrior II pose—a strong standing posture that involves a lot of leg strength and stability—though with my attention scattered. My eyes darting around the room, my to-do list running through my head, my breath shallow. In fact, I've done this many times. Or, I can stand in Warrior II and mindfully set my *drishti* (gaze) on a single point, hone my attention to my measured and deliberate breath, feel the energy spreading from fingertip to fingertip, and engage my core. More and more, as my practice evolves in subtle ways, I go to this place in Warrior II.

My body might look similar in each instance, but the *experience* of the pose is like night and day. The former feels like I'm going through the motions; there but not completely there. The latter feels like my life depends on this very Warrior II. Like it is a precious opportunity. This is bringing the yoga to the yoga posture.

The *Yoga Sutras* is surprisingly quiet on the asana front of the practice. It has much more to say about the yamas and niyamas, for example. However, it does say something about asana that sums up the yogic approach to all forms of movement and, indeed, life itself. Patanjali writes in sutra 2.46: *sthira sukha asanam,* which essentially translates to postures should be performed with effort and ease.

For instance, take a downward-facing dog, probably the most well-known of all of the postures. When you come into a downward-facing dog, it is advised to apply effort by engaging the legs, lifting the sitting bones high, sending the chest wall back towards the tops of the thighs. But, also to apply ease by softening the facial muscles and relaxing the shoulders even as they are working. It's the balance between the two—applying effort in an easeful kind of way—that creates the ideal practice.

This idea of sthira and sukha can be applied to all forms of movement. If you're a runner, of course you need to put forth the effort to keep going, one foot in front of the other, even when it's hard. But that doesn't mean you should ignore its complimentary opposite which is to unfurrow your brow, let your shoulders relax, and unclench your hands. Be alert and engaged without excessive tension and simultaneously be open and relaxed without checking out.

The mindful application of sthira and sukha in our physical movements is beautifully reflective of the yin and yang nature of the world. The sun rises, the sun sets. The tides come in, the tides go out. The seasons arrive, the seasons pass. Every natural phenomenon has its own rhythm. It makes sense, then, that the art and science that is yoga would ask us to do the same with our bodies: find the rhythmic dance of effort and ease. We can take this concept beyond the physical realm too.

In 1996 I was studying my butt off for the California bar exam—the exam you must pass after completing law school if you want to actually practice law. At that time the pass rate was only 60 percent—unusually low for a state bar exam. If you failed, you could take it again. I know some very smart people who took it multiple times. Regardless of smarts though, it's also a pretty stressful thing to go through.

My prep class lasted for months. The exam itself was three excruciatingly long days. I'm not sure I ever studied so hard for anything, and I actually loved to study in high school, college, and law school. I was so stressed out by the volume of material I had to master and the fear of failure that my hair started to fall out and I began to develop an ulcer. It was that bad.

Then, a few days before the exam started I remember a sense of calm coming over me. I had put forth the effort, the sthira. All that was left was to get everything I knew into the little blue notebooks during the exam. A softness then settled in, some sukha. With the effort under my belt, I could ease my way into the exam. I did not feel nervous or anxious. My hair stopped falling out and my stomach settled. I think the element of surrender I was able to bring to the experience really helped. This is just one example of finding the balance between effort and ease in life.

Taking the concept back to the physical practice of yoga, I teach *vinyasa*—a flowing style of yoga that links breath to movement, and one that is physically challenging. I like to teach as well as take difficult classes. I love to get my students sweating and exploring new ways to move their bodies. Some students though fall into the trap of trying to muscle or will their way through so it is fairly common to see these individuals overdoing it and risking hurting themselves. Or even if they are not on the verge of injury, missing the magic that is the sweet balance of effort and ease. Their breathing gets shallow or stuck, their faces turn red from overexertion, and the grunting—let's just say there can be a lot of that.

The well-known yoga teacher Bryan Kest once lamented in a workshop I attended that "students bring their shit into yoga and turn their yoga into shit." What this means to me is that they bring in a sense of competition, a need to put forth 150 percent physical effort every second of the practice, and a self-imposed judgment that if they do not nail every pose or move into the contortions demonstrated by the teacher or other students, then they are not "doing it right." This is where we can see the yoga being lost in the yoga class. "Try easy," a teacher of mine often suggests.

Rolf Gates spent years teaching his students "wise effort" in the face of the extreme over-efforting he saw in his classes. It can take a long time to realize that you don't need to kill yourself on your yoga mat to attain the powerful physical and mental benefits that result from a regular practice. Trying too hard typically has the opposite effect in that we bring our foibles into yoga and mar the beauty and power of the practice itself.

If you practice asana, the next time you unroll your mat for class remember the words *sthira sukha asanam*. Try easy. Bring wise effort to the practice. Surrender a little. You may be surprised to see and feel the joy and sense of radiance that results.

This idea lends itself well to weaving the yamas and niyamas into the asana practice. For example, want to have more compassion? Then practice compassion on your mat; with yourself, whether or not you can stand on your head or balance steadily on one foot; and with those around you in the room, whether or not you find them annoying or distracting in some way. Ahimsa, meet asana, and vice versa.

So you can practice the qualities you want to cultivate in your life right on your yoga mat. It's like your mat becomes your own personal growth laboratory. Say you struggle with impatience. Practice patience on your mat. Notice if you are rushing from pose to pose. See if you can linger in the transitions in between the poses. If you catch yourself mentally planning out the rest of your day, focus on your breath and see if you can stay present without scratching the itch to hurry up and move on to the next thing on your to-do list.

The physical practice is also a great place to play with complementary opposites. Effort and ease; movement and stillness: flowing and then pausing, feeling the pulsation of energy even when your body is still, settling into a steady calmness even when your body is flowing from pose to pose.

Contraction and expansion is another pair of complementary opposites critical to physical well-being. In yoga we learn to hug our muscles in towards our midline, and then expand energy out from our midline. If this sounds really out there, imagine a weight-lifting dude who walks around with hunched shoulders. You can picture it, right? See, he's been engaged purely in contraction. With a yoga practice though, you contract *and* expand. Picture the stereotypical yogi who looks lean and long. There's a suppleness to her spine, an ease in her gait. She's been engaging in the duality that is contraction and expansion.

Many forms of exercise are pure contraction: swimming, running, biking. These are amazing physical activities and if you love them please keep doing them. But also consider adding a little yoga. You knew it was coming, right? The part where I make the case for incorporating the physical practice of yoga into your life? I mean, I'm a yoga teacher.

Now if you have zero interest in the physical practice and just want to learn about the philosophical and contemplative parts of the practice, go ahead and skip the next few paragraphs. You might be sorry you did though because the physical practice of yoga beautifully complements any form of physical activity you can think of, and yields countless health benefits.

I recently chatted with a friend whose daughter runs high school track. She used to be plagued by shin splints. Then she started going to yoga a couple of times a week and the shin splints disappeared. I attribute this to the asana practice using and strengthening parts of the body we didn't even know we had, like the little muscles around the shins that we would never think to work on at the gym.

In addition, evidence-based research on the physical benefits of a regular yoga practice is extensive. The release of our fascia is arguably one of the most important of these benefits. The word fascia means "band" or "bundle" in Latin. Similar to the web-like membrane around each section of an orange, it connects and supports our muscles, ligaments, tendons, organs, and bones.

It is easy to ignore our fascia, as most of us have probably never even heard of it. When we do though, it can become dehydrated and stuck, making us less mobile and less supple. The movements of the asana practice can loosen up and lubricate our fascia. There are specific kinds of yoga practices and techniques that target the release of our fascia, such as yin yoga. Think relaxing the body into a deep stretch for several minutes at a time. Here, the fascial release is facilitated in a way that's like clearing out the cobwebs between our muscles. Thus cleared, the muscles can move more fully and efficiently, increasing range of motion and reducing pain and discomfort. You know how you feel stiff and tight after you've been hunching over your computer or driving for hours? This is an indication that your fascia is stuck.

Even taking a sixty-second break every hour to consciously deepen your breath, stretch your arms overhead, and move your spine side to side can be like hitting the reset button on your body, giving it a little love before diving back into the task at hand. When we find ways to sneak in even tiny bits of movement, we keep our fascia and connective tissue supple. This, in turn, keeps us mobile well into our sunset years. Don't you want to be able to get in and out of a chair or your bed without help when you're in your 80s, 90s, and beyond? Me too.

In addition to keeping our fascia engaged and our muscles lengthened, a regular yoga practice touts almost too many health benefits to count. Improved digestion, better sleep, increased bone health, heightened metabolism, boosted immune function, improved posture, protected cartilage and joints, regulated adrenal glands, and decreased blood pressure, to name just a few.

I imagine now I've at least piqued your interest and you're asking yourself *what kind of yoga should I try?* If your community is anything like mine, there are probably at least half a dozen yoga studios within a twenty-minute drive. Experiment; see what you like. Again, we come back to viveka—discern for yourself which style suits you. And know that this may change as time goes on.

There is no end to the styles of yoga that are widely available: Iyengar, Ashtanga, Power, Restorative, Yin, Vinyasa, and Bikram. Yoga styles range from the serious—Iyengar if you're up for some meticulous alignment instruction—to the silly—"goat yoga." Yes, practicing with goats. I've seen adorable pictures on Facebook of yogis in downward-facing dog while a baby goat tries to climb up their backs. For real.

I encourage you to experiment as if you are testing out seasonings in your favorite soup. You might just discover that you adore cumin, when you never even considered this delicious spice. Go slow, taste a little of this and a little of that. I practically guarantee that you will soon find a style that is delicious.

As important as the style of yoga you find to be right for you is the studio where you feel most at home. Some people may prefer to develop and sustain their yoga practice in the comfort of their own home, using private teachers and/or online resources. Others prefer to studio-hop, not committing to just one place. Both are great options if that speaks to you. For me, having a yoga "home" has been very important. My home has changed over the years. I've enjoyed and learned a ton from the various teachers and studios where I've practiced, and met some of my very best friends along the way.

The studio where I teach (and practice) truly feels like my home away from home. Appropriately, it's named Yoga

Roots. I have really planted and grown there. It's a drama-free sanctuary where everyone is welcome as they are, no questions asked. No matter what's going on in my life, when I walk in the door I get an automatic sense of joy. For me and many others, Yoga Roots is like a healthy version of Cheers: "Everybody knows your name and they're always glad you came."

For so many of us, a sense of community is really important to our well-being. I encourage you to find that for yourself if you are looking to experience yoga in a group setting. I love my time at home, playing alone on my mat. However, there is a communal aspect of the path that feeds my soul—students coming together to support one another as we pursue our individual journeys. Yes, yoga remains an individual journey.

I've been asked more times than I can count if everyone who comes to practice yoga is young and in shape. The answer is no. People of all ages and fitness levels come to Yoga Roots, and that's as it should be. Some only come for the physically more gentle classes like restorative and slow flow. Some come just for the more challenging vinyasa offerings.

Many, including myself, mix and match to cobble together a well-rounded and diversified practice. It's a veritable buffet: take what feeds you, skip what doesn't. And if the studio vibe isn't sitting well with you—I've heard some yoga-curious friends wonder if nearby studios are cliquey or cultish—check around. There's probably another studio nearby that's just what you're looking for.

CHAPTER FOUR
PRANAYAMA – HONORING
YOUR BREATH

I heard a story about the well-know yoga teacher Johnny Kest. He was driving on the freeway with three of his sons. At one point he must have been going too slow for the car behind him because the driver laid on his horn, rolled down his window, and gave Kest the middle finger while screaming obscenities at him. Kest responded by yelling out his own window: "Breathe through your nose!" In yoga philosophy, the practice of breath is considered extremely powerful. It was clearly with this in mind that Kest encouraged "Road Rage Ron" to engage in some conscious breathing to calm himself down.

Prana means life force. While pranayama is all about the breath, the Sanskrit word prana is more encompassing. As the grandfather of modern yoga B.K.S. Iyengar states in *Light on Pranayama*:

"Prana is the breath of life of all beings in the universe. They are born through it and live by it, and when they die their individual breath dissolves into the cosmic breath. Prana is the hub of the Wheel of Life. Everything is established in it."

Our own lexicon shows this to be true as sayings about the breath abound. If something is really beautiful we say, "it's breathtaking." If something touches us immensely we say, "it takes our breath away." If we feel overly excited we say, "we're breathless." Thus, the breath is a powerful metaphor for expressing our emotional realities. All of this points to the potency of the breath, which is something most of us take completely for granted throughout our lives.

From our very first moment on this earth until our last, our breath is always with us. But most of us are largely (or completely) unaware of it. Try this right now. Close your eyes. Notice how your body feels. Label it: tired, stiff, tense, relaxed, etc. Now take five long and slow breaths. Fill up completely as you breathe in. Let all of the air go as you breathe out.

Don't rush through the transitions. Perhaps even find a little pause at the top of the inhale and at the bottom of the exhale. When you're done, notice how your body feels. Has there been a shift? Maybe you feel more awake, more present, more relaxed? If not, that's okay. No pressure or judgment here; just notice. I'd venture to guess that many of you experienced a change for the better, simply from five rounds of breath.

In the asana practice we invariably link our breath to our movements. Body and breath come together in a powerful dance. If you've been to a breath-centered yoga class, you've probably gotten a taste of this. In vinyasa yoga we practice a type of breathing called *ujjayi*. We breathe in and out through the nose, and add a slight constriction in the back of the throat on the exhalation so it can sound a little like Darth Vader. Ujjayi breath translates from Sanskrit as "victorious breath"—it is strong and heat-building, yet also relaxing.

In the *Yoga Sutras* Patanjali describes the breath as being both long and smooth. The key to a proper ujjayi breath is not to try too hard. Remember sthira and sukha; effort and ease. When practiced properly, ujjayi breath has the simultaneous effect of invigorating and soothing. It is helpful to first cultivate your ujjayi breath in a somewhat restful pose, such as child's pose or downward-facing dog. But as the asana practice becomes progressively more challenging, it can be difficult to maintain the smoothness of the breath. If your breathing becomes too labored at some point, if the sthira outweighs the sukha, I encourage you to back off.

The combination of breath and movement can lead to some serious mental and emotional breakthroughs. Certain poses are said to be linked to certain emotions. Hip openers, for example, which typically happen towards the end of a yoga class, are considered storehouses for long-held emotions and even traumas. I've had the experience, as have many of my yogi friends, of settling into a half-pigeon pose, a deep stretch of the outside of the hips, and suddenly noticing tears streaming down my face.

It is really the combination of the physical exertion and the breath work that I've engaged in throughout the class that has lead to these emotional releases. While such an experience can feel scary, especially for the new practitioner who isn't expecting it, it is so healthy to let go in a safe space. To release old tensions and scars, to literally breathe through the emotional maelstrom, and then to walk out of class with a sense of catharsis and ease. That is the power of the breath and movement duo. It is clear that pranayama, the fourth limb of the yoga path, works in concert with the physical postures of the practice. But pranayama also stands on its own.

Modern science is catching up to what the yogis have known for a very long time: the breath is a powerful tool for health and wellness. You've no doubt heard of the fight-or-flight response. It is the body's reaction to a life-threatening situation; one that has withstood the millions of years of human evolution to still be alive and well in each of us now: in prehistoric times it could have been a saber-toothed tiger chasing you through the forest or today it could be an encounter with a hot-tempered person yelling at you.

In those moments it is not the time to methodically weigh your options. It's time to stand your ground or it's time to get the heck out of there. So we don't think, we just act in the way most likely to result in our survival.

When the body kicks into fight-or-flight, we tap into the sympathetic nervous system. The hormone cortisol floods our bloodstream. Our heart rate quickens, our focus narrows, and we virtually go on autopilot. Act now, think later. In times of real emergency, the sympathetic nervous system is where we want to be.

The problem is that many of us spend far too much time in fight-or-flight, practically living there all of the time. As a species we have evolved so that our purpose is not simply to survive and pass on our genes. In that sense, a part of us has moved beyond fight-or-flight. We also need to grow emotionally and spiritually, to live meaningful and fulfilling lives.

However, the chronic stress of our days has many of us stuck in the sympathetic nervous system. Thus, cortisol—aka the "stress hormone"—floods our system habitually. This reality has created a health crisis of sorts. Many doctors consider the ubiquitous nature of cortisol to be "public health enemy" number one. Increased levels of cortisol are causally connected to heart disease, obesity, high blood pressure, sleep disorders, diabetes, depression, decreased bone density, and a decreased immune system, to name just a few maladies. In fact, in 2010 researchers published a study that revealed an increased level of cortisol in heart attack patients as compared to a control group that had lower levels of cortisol and a corresponding lower occurrence of heart attacks.

Conscious breath work can be a powerful antidote to much of this malaise. Through the practice of modulating the breath we can quickly activate the parasympathetic nervous system. Also known as "rest and digest," the parasympathetic nervous system calms the body down and releases the feel-good neurotransmitter serotonin into the bloodstream. This is where we want to spend most of our time if we want to feel vibrant, yet calm.

Furthermore, chronic stress inhibits the production and release of serotonin, whereas being in rest-and-digest increases our serotonin levels. Healthy levels of serotonin enhance feelings of happiness and well-being. They improve our immune system, help us get a good night's sleep, reduce anxiety, and keep our libido strong and our energy high. You may have gotten a little taste of this with the simple deep breaths exercise at the beginning of the chapter.

I understand that it can feel virtually impossible to breathe deeply during moments of stress and anxiety. But I encourage you to try. The next time you find yourself feeling stressed out or anxious, first check in with your breath. I'd venture to guess you will find that it is shallow. It might even feel like you are barely breathing. Then try bringing some effort to your breath. Slow it down. Deepen it. And you will almost certainly feel some immediate relief.

There are fabulous resources on exactly how to engage in pranayama. I highly recommend Donna Farhi's *The Breathing Book* for a deeper exploration of breath work. For our purposes, I'll share a quick and easy exercise that is quite effective at kicking us from fight-or-flight into rest-and-digest. This, like all breathing exercises, is best done in a relaxed seated position. You'll want to sit up nice and tall so that your lungs can expand.

The 4-7-8 Breath

Inhale to a count of four. Hold the breath for a count of seven. Go ahead and count it out silently. Then exhale to a count of eight. Repeat two more times. When our exhales are longer than our inhales, we activate the parasympathetic nervous system. Use this technique once a day for a week and see what you notice. Simply by mindfully attending to your breath, you may be astounded by your newly discovered ability to find calm and ease in the midst of stressful situations.

The word "inspiration" comes from the Latin *inspirare*, which means to breathe spirit into. The etymology here suggests a deep-rooted connection between the physical act of breathing and our spiritual lives. Or, as French philosopher Pierre Teilhard de Chardin said, "We are not human beings having a spiritual experience; we are spiritual beings having a human experience."

Whether or not you believe in God in one form or another, chances are you sense something greater than ourselves. Take a moment to connect to the experience of breathing in and breathing out. Then reflect on the fact that every other living thing on the planet is doing the same. Let your awareness rest in this realization and perhaps even delight in the fact that you are alive.

CHAPTER FIVE
PRATYAHARA – GOING INWARD

The fifth limb of the yoga path is pratyahara, which means withdrawal of the senses. It's about going inward, moving away from the sensory overload that often describes our external world, and getting quiet.

When we engage in pratyahara, we move closer to our inner David. By stripping away our habitual distractions, we get closer to ourselves. As renowned yoga teacher Erich Schiffman said, "Yoga is a way of moving into stillness to discover the truth of who you are." It is this quality of stillness, and its accompanying silence, that characterizes pratyahara.

Ancient yogis practiced pratyahara by going into caves for long stretches and withdrawing from the world. We modern yogis aren't heading for the nearest cave, but this limb is more important than ever in our world of constant stimulation. The digital age is a beautiful, wondrous thing in many respects. All sorts of information is literally at our fingertips; we have the ability to communicate instantaneously with loved ones near and far; we are more informed and in touch than ever—and yet there are serious and worrisome side effects. It seems that our ability to focus attention on one thing at a time is under attack by the technological diversions that are almost always within reach.

We have relatively short attention spans to begin with but in 2000 the average human attention span was twelve seconds. In 2015 it was eight seconds. That is a big drop in a decade and a half. Microsoft published a study to this effect in 2015. The study further found that the human attention span had been eclipsed by that of goldfish. Researchers estimated that the average goldfish can concentrate for nine seconds.

Amy Ippoliti, an incredible yoga teacher and one of the most relevant voices in modern yoga, actually offers a course for yoga teachers on teaching in the digital age. Her aim is to bring the depth of the yoga practice to a population of habitual over-doers and multi-taskers who live as if more is more, but would likely be wiser by understanding that sometimes at least, less is far more.

Recent research suggests that a worker stoned on drugs is more productive than his drug-free colleague doing the same job while multitasking. Even more alarming, at least from a personal fulfillment standpoint, is the statistic that 89 percent of American adults admit to looking at their smartphone during their most recent social interaction and the overwhelming majority of these folks reported that doing so impaired the quality of their conversation. Thus, while we cheer the advent of technology intended to make our lives easier by getting more things done at the same time, in some significant respects it is making our lives worse. We are more distracted, more isolated, and less present than ever before.

Numerous studies also show that social media is wreaking havoc with our self-esteem. There is a great saying: "Don't compare your insides with someone else's outsides." Say you spent an hour putting together "I just threw this on and barely gave any thought to what I look like" attire (don't tell me I'm the only one!) And then Effortless Emily breezes by looking like a million bucks and you wallow in feeling inferior because she obviously does not need to try to look so good. The wise saying suggests you do not compare. After all, what you didn't know is that she just came from the salon and had a professional blow-out.

Or maybe you're in a terrible mood after work and walk into the yoga studio all stressed out praying that you can make it through the 60-minute vinyasa class without completely hyperventilating. And there's Cheery Charlie looking like he was born in the challenging and twisty balancing pose eagle, with a smile on his face to boot. Remember, you have no idea about the inner turmoil he's dealt with or the tortuous path of heartache and loss that preceded this moment in his life. The moral is don't compare.

Social media makes it easy to forget this wise advice. We see people at their absolute best because that's what they've chosen to present. And it's possibly even better than their best with the use of filters that can do everything from lengthen your lashes to shrink your waist, as has become so popular to do in the world of Instagram. And then we compare ourselves and feel unworthy. In fact if you google "Instagram self-esteem," you will instantly be flooded by a slew of articles concluding that our collective self-esteem (women and men, girls and boys) has taken a beating in the world of selfies and glamour shots.

People, myself included, tend to curate their social media profiles. They show themselves and their loved ones on a fabulous vacation, but omit any reference to the penny-pinching and stressing they did to get there. They show themselves looking strong and fit after a workout, but make no reference to the sleeve of cookies they mindlessly consumed the night before while binge watching the latest

Shonda Rhimes series. I don't think it's with bad intent that so many of us curate. After all, I figure that no one really wants to see me looking all haggard and stressed after practically pulling my hair out to meet a deadline on time.

A 2017 *Huffington Post* article entitled *Social Media's Impact on Self-Esteem* reported that based on extensive interviews with men and women ranging from ages 28 to 73, 60 percent of people using social media believed it negatively impacted their self-esteem; and 50 percent believed that their use of social media had negative effects on their relationships. Maybe they were engaging in the online version of "keeping up with the Joneses" or maybe they were feeling less connected with their significant others and friends because of their increasingly persistent state of distraction. Whatever the cause of these statistics, it is clear that when it comes to social media, more is not more.

A few years ago I attended a weekend-long personal growth workshop. It was largely about defining your dreams and then analyzing the ways you stand in the way of achieving them. For a few months thereafter I worked with a life coach who astutely diagnosed me as being "addicted to busyness." Wow, did she nail me. I generally felt good about myself if I had a "productive" day (meaning a busy one).

So if my legal consulting work slowed down and I had nothing needing to be done on a particular day, I would become listless and slightly depressed. This tendency had served me well much of my life. I kept busy and focused on my schoolwork in high school, college, and law school. I did well and went to great schools.

And because of my academic achievements I landed my first real job at a prestigious San Francisco law firm. I practiced employment law at top firms in San Francisco, Boston, and Cleveland for the next eight years. I then took a leap and started my own employment law compliance consulting business helping companies comply with employment laws and create good employee relations. I am now over thirteen years into what has become a fulfilling and, yes, busy business. Thus, the recipe for success of "hard work plus constant stress" plus always be doing something" was pretty well baked into me.

As part of my "treatment" my coach gave me an ingenious daily assignment. She said, "Sit down and do nothing for fifteen minutes a day."

Huh? "I don't understand what you mean."

"Have you ever seen elderly people walking in your nearby park."

"Yes, I have." I love walking in my neighborhood park. "I've got this," I thought.

"Well, have you ever seen them taking a break and sitting on a bench."

"Of course." At this point sweat was starting to form on my palms.

"That's what I want you to do, Sindy. Sit there. Do nothing."

Now at this point I had already developed a pretty solid meditation practice. "So, like, meditate?" I asked hopefully.

"No." She knew that when I set my timer to fifteen minutes to meditate, I felt good because I was accomplishing something, getting to check an item off of my to-do list. She wanted this to be different. To just sit there. Period.

When I shared my assignment with a close friend who was also working with the same life coach, she responded that she was feeling anxious just hearing about it. Nonetheless I did it. At first it felt really awkward. I sat in a chair in my home office and, well, did nothing. I almost felt embarrassed, which was silly since no one else was home, save for my dog Woodrow. In time, I started to look forward to my few minutes of doing nothing. I found I felt refreshed after-wards. Calmer, more present. And when I picked up my to-do list afterwards, I had more energy for what was next. I didn't know it at the time, but I was practicing pratyahara.

Another reason why the thought of getting still and quiet can seem quite daunting is because we worry we won't be able to do it. Not successfully anyway. It is the nature of the mind to wander. To get caught up in stories, rumina-tions, fantasies, and what-ifs. Anyone who has ever sat down to meditate knows this to be true. A 2010 study conducted by psychologists Matthew Killingsworth and Daniel Gilbert found that we spend nearly 50 percent of our waking hours thinking about things that are not related to what we are actually doing in the moment.

The study used the technique of experience sampling where approximately 2,250 subjects were interrupted at random intervals and asked what they were doing, what they were thinking about, and what their emotional state was in that moment. Over a long period of time of gather-ing data, the researchers were able to correlate moments of happiness with behavior and thought patterns. The conclu-sion was clear: "A human mind is a wandering mind, and a wandering mind is an unhappy mind," Killingsworth and Gilbert wrote in the journal *Science.* They continued, "The ability to think about what is not happening is a cognitive achievement that comes at an emotional cost."

Think about this for a moment—it's profound. Our minds wander a significant amount of the time. This is a uniquely human experience. When I look at my dog Woodrow, I know he's not thinking about what he did yes-terday or what he'll be doing tomorrow. He's fully present, at least as much as he can be given his somewhat limited cognitive abilities (my husband has been calling him

"Stupid" for years; Woodrow invariably comes running, tail wagging). We, on the other hand, mentally meander. And this makes us unhappy.

This may seem counterintuitive. For example, what if the activity we are doing honestly is unpleasant? Wouldn't we be happier if we imagined we were lounging on a far-away beach sipping a margarita? The short answer is no.

The researchers found that regardless of what we are doing or what we are thinking about, we are the happiest when our minds are in the present moment. So doing the dishes and being fully present makes us happier than doing the dishes and fantasizing about somewhere we would rather be.

A 2014 study by psychologist Timothy Wilson and colleagues, also published in the journal *Science*, built on Killingsworth and Gilbert's 2010 study and explored why people are averse to being alone with themselves. This study consisted of eleven separate experiments, all of which involved subjects being forced to be alone with themselves—no phones or other distractions—for up to fifteen minutes.

The results were not pretty. Subjects experienced extremely negative feelings. So much so that in one experiment, where subjects were given access to a nine-volt battery capable of administering an unpleasant shock, many chose to shock themselves rather than sit alone with their thoughts. In fact, twelve of the eighteen male subjects and six out of the twenty-four female subjects shocked themselves repeatedly.

These two studies tell a sad story: we habitually engage in mental meandering, which creates suffering. And we loathe being alone with ourselves so much so that we much prefer distractions, sometimes even painful ones. Extrapolating from these results, it is easy to understand why so many of us have literally become addicted to our smart phones. We can always mentally be somewhere else and we never need to be alone. The result is that we suffer.

These studies, and many others like them, are discovering what the yogis have always known. For our own growth and fulfillment, we need to get still, quiet, and present. This is difficult work for most of us. But there is good news. The mind can be trained to be more present. This is the work the ancient yogis engaged in when they retreated to caves for months on end. So we can learn to be comfortable with and even crave the solitude of being alone, sans distractions. Pratyahara is where we begin. We start to withdraw from the external, turn inward, and simply be. Pratyahara is captured perfectly in the old yogi adage: "Don't just do something, sit there!"

The FoMO phenomenon—fear of missing out—is a sense of social angst where we worry that others are having rewarding experiences while we're left out. You might have come across this on Instagram or Facebook—a picture of a group of good looking people having fun at a party, or a selfie of someone post-workout but somehow still looking fresh—and people comment "FoMO!" I imagine you have felt FoMo too. Quite honestly, I have. It's funny, but it's also a little bit sad. We are social creatures and we need community. But, for the good of our own growth, we also need to find solitude; so our fear of missing out can stand in our way.

My husband is a sophisticated litigator who tends to work on bet-the-company kinds of cases. Sometimes he travels a lot, taking depositions and attending hearings around the country. About a decade ago, whenever he would be on a business trip, I would relish the opportunity for some serious GNOs (girls' night out). I'd put my little girl to bed, hire a sitter, and head out the door to hang with my girlfriends.

My husband would inevitably tease me for being such a social butterfly.

During one of his trips I actually went to the same restaurant/bar three nights in a row. A little pathetic, sure, however I didn't want to miss a minute of girl time and being out and about. These days when he travels, I tend to put on my sweatpants by 6 p.m. at the latest and settle in for some solitude—my daughter is now the one who's usually out with friends. I've gotten more comfortable with quiet time and less concerned with who is out with whom and what I might be missing out on. I'm finding pratyahara. Or maybe I'm simply getting old.

As with most things, there is a balance to be struck. You don't want to use pratyahara as an excuse for isolation. Which means sometimes we need to push ourselves to connect with others. Other times we need to push ourselves to disconnect. This is more art than science, to be sure. The practice of yoga in general, and the limb of pratyahara in particular, asks us to discern what we need in any given moment. Self-study (svadhyaya), meet pratyahara, and vice versa.

There's another reason to stop doing and start being. If you're engaged in a creative endeavor of any kind, studies show that boredom is a frequent prerequisite to inspiration and creativity. With technology and its attendant distractions literally at our fingertips every second of every day, we've inadvertently wiped out the *tabula rasa* that is often the springboard to our freshest ideas.

Perhaps you have a complex problem at work to solve. The answer might be to simply let boredom in, thereby creating space for your prefrontal cortex—the part of the brain responsible for problem solving—a chance to churn out some ideas.

We used to have what the experts call "transition zones" between work and home. Baked in periods of quiet, relaxation, and even boredom. We have largely eradicated these with our addiction to smart phones and the like. But we can ease them back into our lives. So the next time you find yourself waiting in a long line at the grocery store, let yourself simply be. Don't pull out the phone to see the latest on Facebook or Snapchat. It may be boring and even uncomfortable, but just let the moment unfold and see what comes up.

Consider how you can find additional pockets of quiet time in your life. If you can swing a silent meditation retreat, all the power to you. Or more simply, pratyahara is within reach right in your own home. When we slow down, get quiet, and go inward, we can get in touch with who we really are. With what is true and beautiful to us. This discernment is an essential part of any path of growth, spiritual or otherwise, plain and simple.

Here are several practices you can consider to introduce some sensory vacation into your days:

- The next time you're in your car don't turn on the music or make a call. Just be with the quiet, without distractions. If the prospect of a silent drive makes you anxious, don't start with the forty-five minute commute. Make your way to the gas station around the block quietly, then give yourself permission to blast some Adele on the way home.
- Take a break from social media. A day, a week, a month; you choose. It will do your mind and spirit wonders. Consider making this a regular thing. One or two days a week, or a few days a month.
- Go a step further and embark on a complete digital detox. No checking your email, newsfeed, or stock

market ups and downs for some period of time. If you need an answer to a burning question, try asking a neighbor instead of Google. If you're not ready to commit to a digital detox, try making just your bedroom a screen-free zone, at least for some set period of time. Notice how much better you sleep. And perhaps notice too how much more engaged you are in other things that take place in the bedroom.

- Try the sit-there-and-do-nothing exercise just as I was assigned by my coach. Even if just for one minute each day, and ideally in nature where you can connect to the physical world around you as you disconnect from the distractions of modern life.

CHAPTER SIX
DHARANA – FINDING THE
POWER OF A FOCUSED MIND

Dharana means concentration. It is a continuation of the process of interiorization of the yoga path, as we practice focusing the mind on one object. Imagine the last time you were so absorbed in what you were doing—something that captivated 100 percent of your attention—that you lost track of everything else around you. Where the only thing that existed for you was the task at hand. This might have happened when you were reading, writing, gardening, practicing yoga, playing tennis, drawing, cooking; the possibilities are endless. Whatever it was you were doing, you were engaged in dharana.

In a yoga class we engage in dharana by focusing our mind on our breath and on the sensations arising in our body. When we do this, the asana practice becomes a moving meditation: Our awareness is fully present. We breathe in, and know that we're breathing in. We breathe out, and know that we're breathing out.

Trust me, it's harder than it sounds. You might begin the class noticing your breath and your body, but before long your mind will likely wander off to *what's for lunch, what did so-and-so really mean when she said such-and-such yesterday, does my butt look fat in these yoga pants, when will the teacher get us out of this damn pose, why can't I look like he does in this posture?* and so on.

In the words of mindfulness meditation teaching giant Joseph Goldstein though, we simply begin again. Your mind wanders; notice that; and come back. Your mind wanders again; notice that; and come back again. Throughout the course of a one-hour yoga class you may do this five hundred times. But don't get upset with yourself—instead, practice ahimsa: self-love and compassion. Just notice, see it for what it is—a wonderfully human distracted mind—and then come back and start again. Breathe in, knowing you're breathing in. Breathe out, knowing you're breathing out.

Along with meditation luminaries Sharon Salzburg and Jack Kornfield, Joseph Goldstein founded the Insight Meditation Society in Barre, Massachusetts. He has studied, practiced, and written extensively about Buddhist-based meditation since the late 1960s. He has led meditation retreats for thousands of students.

Dharana is really the beginning stage of meditation. Any meditation practice asks that we collect and unify our minds; that we concentrate. Since it is impossible to truly concentrate on something and also be mentally meandering, the practice of dharana necessarily takes us into the present moment.

As spiritual teacher Eckhart Tolle expounded on in the best-seller *The Power of Now*, life happens now. End of story. We miss what's happening right before our eyes when we let ourselves get stuck in the past, which already happened, and in the future, which at any given moment is nothing more than fantasy. Tolle accurately observes "there was never a time when your life was not now, nor will there ever be." Dharana helps us with this reality through contributing to firmly rooting us in each present moment as it unfolds.

The use of a mantra is a wonderful way to engage in dharana. A mantra is simply a word or a sound that you say inside your head. It can be as simple as "in" as you inhale and "out" as your exhale. It can be intentional, creating a tool to help cultivate a quality you want more of. Perhaps "I am" on the inhale and "loved" or "safe" or "enough" on the exhale. Though marrying your mantra to your breath is an effective way to keep you centered in the present moment, your mantra does not have to correspond to your breath if that is what you are most comfortable with.

Mahatma Gandhi is best known for his dedication to non-violent resistance and civil disobedience in leading India's peaceful revolution against British colonization. He was peace personified. As yoga teacher and author Stephen Cope relays in his masterful book *The Great Work of Your Life,* there is continuing relevance in today's world for the ancient text of the Bhagavad Gita; a text on which Ghandi based his quest for personal growth. Cope explains:

> "When done systematically, mantra has a powerful effect on the brain. It gathers and focuses the energy of the mind. It teaches the mind to focus on one point, and it cultivates a steadiness that over time becomes an unshakable evenness of temper."

Here Cope is describing the cultivation of becoming a firmly rooted tree. Its branches may sway and even bend with the wind, but they're not going to break off. When we are in this state, we are like Michelangelo hewing closer and closer to David.

Gandhi used a mantra for much of his life. As a boy he was extremely afraid and nervous. And then a family servant schooled him about the power of mantra by suggesting he use *Rama*—the name of a Hindu god—as his own. Ghandi did this for many years. He would recite *Rama* inside his head for hours at a time, often as he walked. What emerged was a steadiness of mind and an inner ease and quiet.

Cope observes: "The mind holds the mantra gently, and it becomes focused, calm, centered." This is dharana, the beginning stage of meditation.

Many years ago a dear friend and teacher taught me mantra-based meditation. She suggested I use the Sanskrit term *so hum*, which translates to "I am that I am." While there are several interpretations for this mantra, which is widely considered a universal sound, it has always had a profound meaning for me: *I am*. I simply exist, end of story. Strip away the labels that adorn me—mother, wife, daughter, sister, friend, yoga teacher and practitioner, lawyer—and there *I am*. There is an inner me that exists apart from my worldly labels, my inner David. I think of this as my soul. I sense into this when I meditate using *so hum*. I say to myself *so* as I breathe in and *hum* as I breathe out.

My mind wanders, sometimes like a puppy dog exploring the outdoors for the first time, and I use my mantra to bring me back just as the puppy's owner gently tugs on the leash to bring the puppy closer in a loving and encouraging way. Remember ahimsa, always ahimsa. So if you are using a mantra and begin to wander, then simply notice this and gently bring yourself back to your mantra. Further, drop the punishing of "I suck at this. Oh my god why can't I just stay with my mantra." Trust me, it's not effective at cultivating the quality of a steady, calm mind.

The use of a mantra need not be limited to the meditation cushion. As Gandhi did, you can use a mantra throughout your day. If you're stuck in traffic or waiting in line at the grocery store, instead of whipping out your phone, consider repeating your mantra in your head. I do this all the time. It's a quick and effective way to center yourself. If you're using an intention-based mantra it is also a great way to feed yourself positive self-talk that can literally change the pathways in your brain.

Science shows that our brains are far more malleable than we thought. Our brains have the quality of neuroplasticity, which means they can continue to change and grow throughout our entire lives. Conventional wisdom twenty years ago was that once you reached adulthood, you were pretty set in your neurological ways. But new research tools, such as functional MRIs, have vastly increased our knowledge about how the brain works and evolves. It turns out you can affect lasting change to the structure of your brain by engaging in various contemplative techniques, like using a mantra, meditating, and engaging in pranayama.

You may, at this point, be rolling your eyes: *C'mon, are you saying that if I walk around all day saying to myself "I am enough," I'll not only start to believe it but I'll actually impact the neurological structure of my brain?*

Yes, I am.

Consider this: if you go the gym every day and do bicep curls, you'd expect to see a change in your biceps. The brain and the mind are not so different. Just two examples relayed in the excellent book *Buddha's Brain: The Practical Neuroscience of Happiness, Love & Wisdom* make this point nicely. Authors Rick Hanson, M.D. and Richard Mendius, Ph.D. cite a study showing that London taxi drivers develop a larger than typical hippocampus, which is the part of the brain mostly responsible for making visual-spatial memories. Since London has a ton of twisty, windy streets, it makes sense that taxi drivers there would need to remember a lot in a visual sort of way and thus their brains adapt to accommodate that need.

Hanson and Mendius also cite a 2004 study by world-renowned neuroscientist Richie Davidson that found when one becomes happier, the left frontal region on the brain becomes more active. Thus, they conclude "what flows through your mind sculpts your brain." Accordingly, by applying some effort to what flows through your mind— and use of a mantra or engaging in the other meditation techniques described in this book is an excellent way to accomplish this—you can actually rewire your brain for the better. Like going to the gym, this rewiring only occurs with consistent effort and practice.

Perhaps you've heard this metaphor: while drops of water don't have much impact on the terrain, over the course of hours, days, months, and years repeated drops of water can carve canyons. This point really applies to all of the steps along the path of yoga. The yamas and niyamas, asana and pranayama practice, and so on. Small actions we take and changes we make can have tremendous and lasting impacts that truly shape the terrain of our lives. Transformation does not happen all at once or with a big downpour. It happens one drop of water at a time.

There's a great line in the movie *Spiderman* that my husband loves to quote. Uncle Ben tells a young Peter Parker "Remember, with great power comes great responsibility." His words are apt here. Knowing that you have the power to literally change your brain, I encourage you to do so in a way that is consistent with your personal growth and spiritual goals. If you want more love and peace in your life, you can cultivate it with your self-talk and mantra. Just as you wouldn't plant an apple seed and expect a banana tree to grow, it is just as implausible to tell yourself you suck and expect self-love to grow.

Let's take a step back and remember *why* we want to love ourselves: to heal, to be of service to others, and to spread more love and peace in the world, just to name a few reasons. It's not selfish to take care of yourself from the inside out; to attend to your emotional well-being and to detach from your daily stressors. In fact, it's selfish not to. If you don't, how can you show up fully for those in your life? You can't, at least not in an effective way. Just as it's true that you can't heal yourself from a place of self-flagellation and negative inner dialogue, you also cannot be there for others if you are not first taking care of yourself.

Self-care is a big buzzword in the healing professions. At the Cleveland Rape Crisis Center it's something the board speaks of often with respect to the staff—especially regarding those on the front lines working with victims of sexual assault. Research tells us that these rape counselors, along with first responders and others working with victims who have suffered trauma, can take on some of the suffering of their clients because they empathetically engage with them. While this empathetic engagement helps them do their job well, it can also cause them distress. Thus, to be able to continue to do the important work they do, these caregivers have to actively engage in caring for themselves. Otherwise, burnout is likely to ensue. And when that happens, they can no longer effectively support the healing of others.

Whether or not you work closely with others who have suffered, it's critically important that you take care of yourself. You have an inner David. You *are* an inner David. Go on and keep chipping away at all that which is not your David. Our world needs the real you, perhaps now more than ever before.

CHAPTER SEVEN
DHAYANA – CREATE AND
SUSTAIN A MEDITATION
PRACTICE

There's so much hype about meditation these days. It seems as if every week there's a new meditation app or another story in the news about the myriad physical and emotional benefits from meditating. This is an exciting time.

For the ancient yogis, meditation *was* yoga, plain and simple. Asana practice was just a practical means to an important end. Asana was to make the body vibrant and supple enough so that yogis could sit and meditate comfortably for hours on end. Literally, that was the point of asana. To be able to sit comfortably for hours in meditation.

The world of modern postural yoga has, in many respects, moved away from yoga's deeply rooted commitment to meditation. If you look up "yoga" or popular hashtags on Instagram like "#yogaeverydamnday" and "#yogaeverywhere," you'll be searching for a very long time to find anyone sitting in meditation. Instead you're likely to see fancy poses in scenic settings. Which is cool, but it's slightly misleading. Yoga is not just about, or even primarily about, the poses. If you want to take a deep dive into this thing called yoga, meditation is where it's at.

What exactly does it mean to meditate? Definitions abound but for our purposes let's consider meditation to be *the practice of turning one's attention inward to see the contents of the mind with a friendly but detached attitude.* My practice is to sit on my meditation cushion in a comfortable cross-legged position. I also sit up with a tall spine so that my breath can flow easily. Then I gently close my eyes and, if I'm using a mantra, begin to recite *so hum* in time with my breath. I notice my thoughts as they come and as they go. I often get carried away with them, but when I notice that I've engaged with my thoughts, I gently bring myself back to my mantra and my breath. I don't get mentally churned up when my thoughts wander, as I know that's simply the nature of the mind. Instead, I remind myself to come back to my breath and mantra. And yes, this can be very difficult to do.

Keep in mind that what I just described is simply one way to meditate. There are literally more ways to meditate than I can count. But before we go further into this discussion on meditation, I'd like to debunk some common meditation myths.

Meditation Myth #1: You have to sit in a pretzel-like shape and keep perfectly still while you meditate. This is false. I'm certified to teach mindfulness-based meditation through The Mindfulness Center in Bethesda, Maryland. As its name suggests, the center works to bring mindfulness practices to the world of healthcare and beyond. Its premise is that health and well-being are within reach for each of us if we learn to engage in mindfulness-based self-care.

The center's founder, neuroscientist Deborah Norris, teaches meditation by first telling her students to get comfortable. They can sit, they can recline, they can do something in between. They can even stand if they like. Most of the center's students lay down to meditate. However, many meditation teachers, including Joseph Goldstein, teach their students to begin seated. You can experiment with what works for you; it is advised though that a top priority be settling in with what is comfortable for you. And if discomfort creeps in during the meditation, by all means move around so you can get comfortable.

What if you get so darn comfortable that you fall asleep? Opinions vary on this one. I've heard meditation teachers advise that if you fall sleep, you obviously needed to sleep so enjoy the nap and try again tomorrow. Others suggest you'll miss the point if you fall asleep, so be careful not to get too comfortable. This is really about experimentation and finding what works for you. When I teach meditation, most of my students lay down. Others like to meditate while sitting in a comfortable chair. Personally I prefer to meditate sitting on my very worn in meditation cushion with an upright spine. But again, this is about experimenting and finding what's right for your own practice.

Meditation myth #2: The correct way to meditate is to completely clear your mind. Lucky for me and probably for all of you, this too is false. When we meditate, we come into the seat of the witness. We watch our thoughts and mental machinations without trying to control them, and then we simply return to our point of focus, be it the breath, a mantra, or the sensations in the body. By simply watching in this manner, we begin to identify as the observer, seeing our thoughts as the observed. We learn that we are not our thoughts. Our thoughts will arise, they will abide, and they will dissolve. We—the observer, the seer, the witness—remain. This recognition is like taking a chisel to the stone that surrounds our inner David as we get closer and closer to the truth of who we really are. Pure awareness, as some call it.

You may find fleeting moments of a relatively clear mind when you meditate. And then again, you might not. It's all okay. The goal is not to have no thoughts. Rather, it is simply to be accepting and patient with whatever comes to your mind. To see it, not cling too tightly to it, and let it go.

Meditation myth #3: You must meditate for hours to reap any benefits from the practice. Nope, not the case. I have a friend named Joe who I met during my first teacher training. Joe came to yoga via meditation, which is unusual. Typically, as was the case for me, the practitioner finds asana first. Then, falling in love with yoga, they feel compelled to find the deeper, more contemplative aspects of the practice and thus discover meditation.

I also host a book club at Yoga Roots where we do two of my favorite things. Read books about yoga and then talk about them. It's a great way to nerd out on this stuff with other like-minded geeky yogis. Joe is a regular and has made many unforgettable comments in our book club. Once he said, "Yoga isn't about getting a nice ass, it's about getting your head out of your ass." That was a keeper. And as my stepdaughter pointed out, these need not be mutually exclusive. Joe also relayed that in talking to students about meditation he advises them to breathe mindfully for one breath. Breathe in and know you're breathing in. Breathe out and know you're breathing out. Do this once. Maybe work your way up to five breaths. It's a wonderful, accessible way to introduce the practice.

Here's the thing. You can actually reap the benefits by meditating for one breath. Now you won't get as many benefits as you would if you had an hour-long daily practice, or as many benefits if you had a twenty-minute daily practice (which is around where I hover). But you will get a sense of being connected to yourself and the present moment in a way that you may find quite powerful. It might feel really good, so good that you decide to stay a few more minutes. Even a minute a day is solid. I suggest you start with a breath and work your way up. As you learn to meditate for longer periods of time, you may find you go deeper, you may even find pockets absent of thoughts, where instead of thinking, you simply exist.

It is helpful to set up a spot where you can meditate regularly. I have a little corner of my home office with my cushion and other meditation goodies. Some beads, some essential oils, and some other yogi tchotchkes so that when I come to my cushion I have a Pavlovian-like response. I instantly feel calmer, more centered. My breath starts to deepen. My environmental cues let me know it's time to get a little Zen.

Meditation myth #4: It's self-indulgent to meditate. I never considered this a barrier to meditation but apparently it stands in the way of developing a practice for many people. I know this from Dan Harris. Let me tell you a thing or two about Harris, an ABC newscaster. He was introduced to meditation circa 2004, after he had a panic attack on live television. The attack was a major catalyst in his life. Not only did he embark on a journey of self-awareness and personal growth, he also wrote a *New York Times* bestselling book about it—*10% Happier: How I Tamed the Voice in My Head, Reduced Stress Without Losing My Edge, and Found Self-Help That Actually Works*—and founded a companion podcast and app. Harris is truly one of my favorite people. Though we've never met and he has no clue I exist, I think if he got to know me, we'd be tight.

Harris is funny as all get-out, extremely self-deprecating—a trait I insist on in all my close peeps—smart, articulate, warm, and kind. He's the real deal. In *10% Happier* he articulates a vision that he came upon during his own journey: a world in which meditation is socially acceptable and not considered weird or out there. He states, "I pictured a world in which significant numbers of people were 10% happier and less reactive. I imagined what this could do for marriage, parenting, road rage, politics—even television news." It's not too lofty, this vision, and quite within reach. We certainly have a ways to go. Politics right now, for example, have never been more rancorous or downright nasty in my lifetime. But I, like Harris, am hopeful.

Not too long ago he embarked on a bus tour around the country with meditation teacher Jeff Warren (no relation, sadly). The two talked to people about meditation everywhere they went. They wanted to share the wealth that can arise from a regular meditation practice and also to get a sense of why so many people don't do it. One theme that emerged was that people view the whole self-care/personal growth thing as selfish. Their lives are busy. They've got things to do, people to take care of. Here's what I, and many others, say to that: "Put your own oxygen mask on first." This may be a somewhat tired metaphor, but it's used so often for a reason: it's right on. If you are not in a good place—physically, emotionally, spiritually—you cannot be there in a healthy way for anyone else. Mic drop.

Even more ubiquitous than the meditation hoopla that surrounds us is the trending "mindfulness." We hear it all the time, advertisers market it to us (mindful muffins anyone?) and pop culture magazines lead with it. But what is it? Harris literally draws an illustration of it on the *10% Happier* app: Picture a waterfall. Our thoughts, emotions, and reactions comprise the waterfall. Mindfulness, per Harris, is what exists behind the waterfall. Seeing it and observing it, yet somehow being separate from it. Many of my students and I find this visualization extremely helpful when it comes to understanding what we are trying to do when we engage in mindfulness meditation. We see and observe the waterfall, yet at the same time we know that we are not the waterfall.

Armed with this metaphor, and with the profound knowledge that we are not our minds, we can begin to find some detachment from our racing thoughts, emotions, and reactions. From this place of observation and detachment, we can make wiser choices; choices that serve us and the betterment of the world.

For example, when the thought arises *I must have another piece of chocolate cake ASAP,* we can better see it for what it is. Simply a thought. We need not be enslaved by it. By creating this space between what arises (the sense of craving, the belief that you need the cake) and how we react to it (eat now think later, or observe without reaction and perhaps opt to hold off on slice number two), we give ourselves more options.

A yoga and meditation practice offers us healthy tools to create space between stimulus and response; between what arises in our lives and how we react to it. I think back to my earlier tendency to beep the horn at the poor guy or gal in the car in front of me who didn't immediately step on the gas when I wanted them to. It used to feel like I had no choice. I encountered stimulus—annoyance at the slow driver—and I reacted.

Through my practice though, I learned to create space. The annoyance still arose, and for a long time I still wanted to beep, but I restrained myself. It was a process. Nowadays, the stimulus of a slower driver rarely registers even a blip.

That's a simple example of the power of the practice and demonstrates the cultivation of the ability to respond, not merely to react. If I sound more advanced in my personal journey than I actually am, let me keep it real. Occasionally I still want to beep at the car in front of me, for no good reason other than it's not going as fast as I would like it to. And occasionally, I actually do so. Also, on occasion I long for the second piece of cake even though I'm already full and know it will make me feel crappy. Yet, sometimes I eat it.

As yoga teachers often say, it's called a "practice" for a reason. If it were called yoga perfect, I'd have given up a long time ago. What keeps me going though is the knowledge that when I look at my foibles and imperfections with gentler eyes, I am better able to move on quickly and hopefully make healthier, more compassionate choices.

There is also more to mindful eating than simply foregoing an overindulgence that might taste good in the moment but is sure to make you feel regret after the "treat" has passed your lips. Research shows that restrictive dieting is not the way to health and/or weight loss, at least not in a sustainable way. The way to create optimum health is to eat a balanced, clean diet. This means, in the words of *Food Rules* author Michael Pollan, "Eat food, not too much, mostly plants." If your diet contains large amounts of pre-packaged foods with ingredients you cannot pronounce, I suggest you look at your diet more closely. For the most part, I suggest you eat whole foods found in nature. In addition, as important or even more important than *what* you eat is *how* you eat. Eating mindfully is a skill you can cultivate, and many studies have shown that mindful eating is a huge contributor to overall wellness.

There are three key steps to eating mindfully. First, eat without distractions. If you are eating alone, see if you can just eat and not do something else at the same time. Remember the definition of Zen is doing one thing at a time. Eat, and know that you are eating. Really taste the food. Notice and appreciate the texture and the smell of each bite. I'm not going to lie, this is exceedingly hard for me. When I eat alone, I am often also reading or working. My "I should be doing something productive" hardwiring is really difficult for me to overcome. If you have this problem too, I suggest you start small. Maybe even just with the first three bites of your meal. Now if you're dining with others it can be even more difficult to focus on what you're eating and how it tastes. So just remind yourself to compassionately take notice.

Second, slow down. The slower you eat, the more time you give your body to catch on to the fact that it is being nourished. When you eat fast, you almost always eat more than you need. It typically takes about twenty minutes for feelings of satiety to travel from stomach to brain. So if you eat too fast you can miss the cue that you've had enough.

Third, take a moment to think about the wonder that is the food in front of you. Imagine the path it took to find its way to your plate. I encourage you to express gratitude for your bounty.

What kind of meditation practice is right for you? It will likely take some experimentation to find out, unless you hit on a method that instantaneously resonates with you.

I highly recommend you try some or all of the following three techniques. And then follow up with an experienced meditation teacher or signing up for the *10% Happier* app or some other meditation tool that resonates with you.

● Mantra-based meditation

We've covered this one. You can use something as simple as "in" as you inhale and "out" as you exhale. Or you can get more intentional about it. Start with "I am" on the inhale and pick a word on the exhale. As I suggested earlier "enough," "loved," and "safe" are effective. A fellow meditation teacher I've practiced with often instructs her students to use "I am" on the inhale and "here" on the exhale. "I am here" is a lovely centering and grounding mantra.

If you are creating an intention-based mantra, I suggest sticking with it for some period of time. Let it really sink in. Digest it, if you will, before considering moving on to another one.

Another way to engage in a mantra-based meditation is through the use of mala beads. You may have seen yoga teachers and practitioners wearing long strings of beads, either around their necks or wrists. These are likely mala beads, a strand of 108 beads used for keeping count in mantra meditations. The number 108 is an auspicious one in yoga. Explanations abound for the significance of the number, but one popular explanation is that the number one stands for the universe; the number zero represents the humility that is required in any spiritual practice and the number eight stands for infinity and timelessness, much like the eight-limbed path itself.

To use mala beads for meditation, take a comfortable seated position while holding your mala in your right hand, draped between your middle and index fingers. Starting at the guru bead—the larger bead—use your thumb to count each smaller bead, pulling it towards you as you recite your mantra. Do this 108 times, traveling around the mala until you reach the guru bead again.

Using mala beads for meditation can lend the practitioner a lovely sense of satisfaction. When I use mala beads and touch that last bead under my thumb, I feel like I've completed something important. Mala beads are almost as ubiquitous as yoga pants. Google them and see what appeals to you aesthetically. Mala beads can also be used as an intention setting tool. You see, certain stones and materials are said to have specific meanings. For example, mala beads made of jade are considered to combine the qualities of wisdom and tranquility. Mala beads made of rose quartz are considered to invite in unconditional love and heart opening. There's almost no end to the designs and stated intentions of mala beads.

- Mindfulness meditation

This is primarily where the current meditation buzz is at. Here's the skinny on how it's done: take a comfortable position and close your eyes. Start to turn your gaze inward by noticing your breath. Notice too the sensations of your body. Our bodies hold on to a lot of emotional tension. Maybe in the shoulders, the hips, the back, even the jaw. See if you can relax the tension, and then come back to noticing your breath. When a sensation in your body calls attention away from your breath, make a soft mental note. Something like "tension" or "pressure." When it passes, it's back to the breath. That's it!

I am a big fan of Insight Timer, a free app that has lovely Tibetan bowl-like chimes that indicate when it's time to begin and end your meditation. It also shows you how many other people around the world are meditating at that moment using the same app. It's a cool feeling to finish even just a five-minute meditation and see that "you just meditated with 3,967 people." It gives me a sensation of being connected to like-minded peeps near and far.

Per Dr. Norris of the Mindfulness Center, there are two key ingredients in mindfulness meditation. The first is interoceptive awareness. You may have heard the term proprioception: this is knowing where your body is in time and space. Lebron James is a stellar example of demonstrably high proprioception. Watch him handle the basketball and you can witness that he knows exactly where he is on the court—every inch of him, every second.

For us mere mortals, the asana practice is an effective way to increase our proprioception. By tuning into our bodies on our yoga mats, we feel into precisely where we are. For example, in the balancing pose called half-moon—Ardha Chandrasana if you want to get all Sanskrit about it—your left leg is to be aligned with your left hip. For years when I did this pose I assumed my left leg was appropriately lined up. Then a skilled teacher adjusted me a few times and I sensed where my leg actually was—a few inches out of alignment. It was a great learning process for me in enhancing my proprioceptive awareness.

Interoceptive awareness though is becoming skilled at knowing what's going on inside your body. For example, emotions can hide away. So by developing awareness of what you are actually feeling on the inside, you actually cue your body to initiate any healing that needs to take place.

In her book *In the Flow*, Dr. Norris shares the most recent research on meditation and healing: Studies show that mindfulness meditation—where we attend to the sensations of the body, including painful ones—helps us both cope with pain and cure the underlying cause. Let me explain. When you feel safe, your body can relax and activate the parasympathetic nervous system. Then, feeling into areas of discomfort or pain, your brain literally begins to regulate your body's healing processes.

Dr. Norris conducted her own related research at the Veteran Affairs Medical Center in Washington D.C. She introduced patients that had been injured during their service to our country to mindfulness meditation. She first guided them into a state of relaxation and then guided them to sense the physical pain that was plaguing them. For the first week or two many of the veterans reported an increase in their pain. They were feeling their bodies, when before they were ignoring their bodies and trying to shut out the pain.

Then within eight weeks, a statistically significant number reported that their physical pain was completely gone. These were individuals who had tried many other kinds of medical interventions to alleviate their physical pain. But nothing worked—that is until they created and sustained a practice of mindfulness meditation. Norris's research, as well as that of many others, proves the old yogi adage "You need to feel to heal."

The second ingredient in mindfulness meditation is compassion. If you tune in to your body, breath, and mind with a gentle mental attitude you can quickly begin to see the benefits of the practice. However, if your approach is antagonistic, critical, and judgmental, you likely set yourself up for frustration and even inertia.

Remember, you simply cannot grow and enhance your skillfulness at dealing with life when you hate on yourself. So when engaging in a mindfulness meditation practice, I strongly encourage you to go easy on yourself; to approach yourself as you would your very best bestie. This will naturally translate to how you show up in your life. Again, you hew closer to your inner David.

● Metta meditation

Metta means loving-kindness in Sanskrit. It's an increasingly popular style of meditation where the practitioner systematically sends good wishes to himself and to others. It definitely can feel warm and fuzzy, perhaps even downright silly, especially at first. However, it is considered an extremely powerful tool to cultivate the quality of compassion. I first learned about Metta meditation from my yogi friend Joe. He shared the following words and suggested I read them at first until I had them memorized:

May I be happy. May I be healthy. May I be safe. May I walk through the world with ease.

May those for whom compassion comes easy for me be happy. May those for whom compassion comes easy for me be healthy. May those for whom compassion comes easy for me be safe. May those for whom compassion comes easy for me walk through the world with ease.

May the strangers in my life be happy. May the strangers in my life be healthy. May the strangers in my life be safe. May the strangers in my life walk through the world with ease.

May my enemies be happy. May my enemies be healthy. May my enemies be safe. May my enemies walk through the world with ease.

May all beings be happy. May all beings be healthy. May all beings be safe. May all beings walk through the world with ease.

Meditation teacher and co-founder of the Insight Meditation Center in Barre, Massachusetts Sharon Salzberg is widely considered a leading expert in Metta meditation. In her newest book, *Real Love,* she explains that when we engage in Metta meditation we literally exercise the part of the brain where compassion resides and practice makes it stronger. True compassion is not akin to the cliché of the purple Barney character belting out "I love you, you love me, we're a happy family." Thankfully, it's really not like that at all.

Compassion is a state a mind, an attitude we cultivate where we relate both to ourselves and to those around us with a sense of interconnectedness. We don't assume the pain of others in a way that drains us; rather, we approach our world with an open heart. When we do so, we benefit even more than the objects of our compassion. Research also shows that loving-kindness meditation increases our vagal tone, the neural connection between the brain, heart, and other organs. This, in turn, facilitates the release of the feel good hormone oxytocin, which reduces blood pressure and inflammation while strengthening our immune systems.

In addition to the physical benefits that inure to practitioners, Metta meditation has been shown to yield transformative mental and emotional benefits. So many of us walk around in a state of emotional contraction. Protecting ourselves from hurt and thus being closed off from the possibility of true connection. When we work to strengthen our "compassion muscle," we lean into a sense of emotional expansion. We experience heartfelt warmth for others and in that way open ourselves to more authentic relationships.

While engaging in Metta meditation may feel forced and even phony at first, it's widely considered to be a powerful practice that progresses quickly from the silly to the profound. I suggest you try it. After all, what have you got to lose?

I heard a great interview recently on the *10% Happier* podcast (I know, I'm mildly obsessed). Harris spoke with his ABC colleague Robin Roberts, who is also a dedicated meditator. She, and indeed many famous people from all walks of life, practice a kind of meditation called Transcendental Meditation, or TM for short. TM involves meditating with a given mantra for twenty minutes every morning and twenty minutes every evening.

To partake, you need to take a course where you will be assigned a personal mantra in Sanskrit. Roberts described an amazing conversation she had with her teacher about the process. They were discussing the sometimes frustrating ebbs and flows in a meditation practice. Some days a meditation practice can feel amazing. You feel in the zone, at one with yourself and everything else, and like you could sit comfortably for hours. Other days though are just the opposite. You struggle with a racing mind or emotional upset. Ten minutes feels like ten hours.

Roberts's teacher described that there is a deep end of the meditation pool and a shallow end. Sometimes the practitioner will go deep—some seasoned meditators can even hang out in the deep end all the time. While sometimes the practitioner will stay in the shallow end, trying mightily to return to breath or mantra again and again. But either way, everybody gets wet. Shallow end, deep end, we're all in the water. I find this to be a reassuring explanation. Our time spent meditating—whether we think we're nailing it or no—is not time wasted at all. The practice will bear fruit, whether a mere apple or an entire orchard.

CHAPTER EIGHT
SAMADHI – FINDING THE
ULTIMATE CONNECTION

Samadhi is often translated as enlightenment. This is the ultimate goal of the eight-limbed path, according to the ancient yogis. Samadhi is not a state you attain and remain in. Rather, you find moments of it along your journey. Perhaps while meditating, or practicing yoga on your mat, or walking along the beach, or standing among the trees, or watching a sunset, or gazing up at the stars, and feel yourself connected with all things.

Rolf often says we, as individuals, are like waves that have forgotten we are part of the ocean. In Samadhi, you realize that you *are* the ocean. This analogy speaks to an important point in yoga philosophy, namely that any perceived separation between us is illusory. We are all connected; we are all one. This is what the closing salutation in yoga class, Namaste, means.

One translation of Namaste that I'm exceedingly fond of is this: "I honor that place in you where the whole universe resides. And when I am in that place in me, and you are in that place in you, there is only one of us." This speaks to our interconnectedness. Perhaps a more accessible way to think of this can be found in the poignant words in Maya Angelou's poem *Human Family*:

"I note the obvious differences between each sort and type, but we are more alike, my friends, than we are unalike. We are more alike, my friends, than we are unalike. We are more alike, my friends, than we are unalike."

When we get out of our own heads and our own ways and really listen to our own hearts, we might begin to sense into this truth.

The final pose in every yoga class is the resting posture called Savasana, or Corpse Pose. You lay on your back with your eyes closed and let yourself sink into your mat; rest easy, let go of any effort or holding on. Metaphorically speaking, Savasana is where you dissolve your limiting beliefs about yourself and your place in the world. It is where we have the opportunity to be reborn to our highest selves and to know the truth of Rumi's words: "We are not a drop in the ocean; we are the entire ocean in a drop."

Lest we throw up our hands in despair at the seemingly out-of-reach limb of Samadhi, I think it is very important for the modern yogi to not get too caught up in attainment of any kind. We modern yogis must realize that being on the path, at whatever stage we find ourselves in, is where we find the juice.

So I suggest: think more journey, less destination. And through the journey—where you engage in the seeming paradox of simultaneously working on yourself and loving yourself—you can come into a place where you live with an open heart and a present mind. From this place, you are of service to those around you. Your service might simply consist of showing up as the best version of yourself. It might be your ability and willingness to offer a safe and healing space for a hurt loved one. Or it could be giving back to the world by engaging in volunteerism or philanthropy of some kind. The possibilities are literally endless.

"Enlightened" is not a word I would ever use to describe myself. Those who know me would undoubtedly agree. But my years on the path of yoga have drawn me closer to my inner David. There is, and always will be, more work for me to do; which is how it should be for almost all of us. But the countless hours I've spent on my yoga mat, or on my meditation cushion, or reading about, talking about, learning about, or otherwise engaging with the path have born significant fruit. I am not the same woman I was before I began my journey. I am more content, more clear about what I value, more introspective in a gentler way. That is the gift the path of yoga has brought me.

Samadhi just might be where, on your own path, you can feel into the idea that you are okay just as you are, with whatever comes up. Even just by stepping into nature and feeling a sense of awe at its vastness and beauty, you might sense the connectedness of all living things, while also knowing you are a special part of this union. With this knowledge, and a sense that you are already complete, imagine the peace and radiance you could share with your small corner of the world.

CHAPTER NINE
THE SEVEN CHAKRAS AND
THE EIGHT-LIMBED PATH

I have a young friend who participates in the yoga book club that I mentioned earlier. She asks the most insightful questions that belie her age. One Saturday evening, this eighteen-year-old gem texted me to ask how my evening was going.

"Great," I responded as I was out with my husband and some friends enjoying a cocktail and a nice dinner.

"Question: how do the chakras fit into the eight-limbed path of yoga?" she texted back.

Izzy, this chapter is for you.

The chakras, of which there are seven, are considered to be energy centers along the spine. Rolf uses the chakras in his teacher trainings as a kind of map of psychodynamic personal development. In my advanced teacher training with him I was assigned numerous papers to write on the chakras, so one day as I was working away on one, my then-tween daughter asked me what I was doing.

I started to describe the chakras to her but she quickly interrupted—

"Mom, if you take an X-ray of the spine can you see the chakras?"

"Um, no."

"Then they're not real," she proclaimed and walked away.

I understand this may not be your jam. However, the chakras are nearly as entrenched in this thing called yoga as a downward facing dog. Actually, many yogis consider the chakras not only real, but critically important to over-all health and well-being. The word chakra literally means wheel—imagine a vortex of spinning energy at various points along the spine with each of these energy centers corresponding to physiological and neurological systems in the body. Each also has personal growth and spiritual implications. Thus, when your chakras are not healthy, you may suffer physical ailments as well as emotional upset. The good news is a balanced yoga practice helps keep your chakras open and aligned.

The first chakra sits right at the tailbone. It's called the root chakra, or *Muladhara* in Sanskrit. Each of the chakras is associated with a color; the root chakra's is red. This first chakra aligns with tribal allegiances, and childhood senses of security or lack thereof. When you are in balance in the root chakra you feel stable and grounded. When you're not, you tend toward the flighty and scattered. Most yoga classes begin by addressing the root chakra in that we start from a fairly effortless resting posture that is close to the ground. I typically ask my students to feel into a sense of ease and safety at the beginning of an asana practice.

In *Anatomy of the Spirit*, author Carolyn Myss asks the reader to tap into their root chakra by imagining a time when something "tribal" touched them in an emotional way. Upon reading this, what immediately came to my mind was then-President Obama's speech at the Democratic National Convention in July 2016.

In explaining what makes America so special he spoke about our collective power to shape the world in which we wish to live. To come together to reject tyranny, to affirm equality and justice for all, and to bring to life the words of the Declaration of Independence "that all men are created equal." I felt chills listening to that speech. I felt a sense of belonging and purpose; a sense of shared values, of inclusion, equality, and justice. This was root chakra territory for me.

Next along the spine is the sacral chakra, or *Svadhisthana*. Sitting at the low back and abdomen, this chakra is orange and is concerned with personal relationships. Myss states: "the spiritual challenge of the second chakra is to learn to interact consciously with others: to form unions with people who support our development and to release relationships that handicap our growth."

We have all spent time here, working our way through and hopefully out of unhealthy relationships, opting instead for more supportive and growth-oriented ones. The second chakra is also considered the home of creativity. I've never really considered myself a creative person. However when I roll out my yoga mat and invite my body to move, I find that my postural creativity flows.

The third chakra is located at the solar plexus, that space between the navel and ribs. Called the *Manipura* chakra, this bright golden yellow-hued hub is considered the home of your personal power. It is where you make life choices that support your growth, and act with courage and ambition. It is also where you cultivate self-acceptance and love. If the first chakra is about how you relate to the group and the second chakra is about how you relate to your significant others, the third chakra is all about how you relate to yourself. Myss puts it this way:

"The energies that come together in this chakra have but one spiritual goal: to help us mature in our self-understanding—the relationship we have with ourselves, and how we stand on our own and take care of ourselves."

Imagine a time when you put yourself first; not in a selfish way but in an empowering way. My first marriage looked perfect. We appeared to be so compatible and successful. Why would I leave such a great guy from such a great family and with so much to look forward to? From the outside it looked like we had it all going on: professionally, socially, materialistically. But I was not in any way standing in my own power. Quite the opposite; I was subjugating that which supported my growth for that which was expected of me. To look, sound, act, even vote a certain way.

I have always had left-leaning political views and I care deeply about equality for women, minorities, LGBT, and any other oppressed groups. I grew up in a largely Democratic suburb outside of Hartford, Connecticut, went to Tufts University near Boston for my undergraduate degree and Stanford Law School for my law degree.

Liberal values were baked into the fabric of where I lived and studied; they were always intrinsic to my surroundings and my sense of self. During my first marriage, circa 2000, my husband's family made it clear that they expected us to vote for a presidential candidate who would be better for them in terms of their tax obligations. Yet, their candidate was not much of a supporter for the values I held most dear to my heart. Nonetheless, I bought into their storyline and reasoned *my in-laws are "generous" with us so I owed it to them to at least vote as they wish.* I am embarrassed and ashamed to admit that I went behind the curtain, into the voting booth, and did what was expected of me.

Soon after though I experienced sharp waves of cognitive dissonance. You know, the sense you get when you have a belief and then take an action that contradicts that belief. It's an uncomfortable feeling, to put it mildly, and one that hastened the end of my marriage. You may have heard the saying "death by a thousand cuts." My willingness to compromise my core societal values for the sake of supposed familial harmony was just one such cut that contributed to my divorce a few short months later. The voting decision was mine, not my ex's or his family's. They are not to blame for what I did behind the curtain; I am.

However, the whole situation made clear to me that I could not grow or authentically live in the context of my marriage. I've also looked at this as a battle of the chakras. Left-leaning political and societal values: root chakra. Family loyalty: root chakra. Marriage to law school sweetheart: sacral chakra. Allegiance to myself, my heart and my own growth: solar plexus chakra. I chose one variant of my root chakra and really stepped into my third chakra with a sense that I was righting my own ship.

There were consequences. My family and many of my friends were completely baffled by my seemingly hasty decision. I recall a friend crying on the phone to me, saying, "If you couldn't make it, how can any of the rest of us stand a chance?" And our "couple friends" quickly dispersed. Lawyer colleagues from work looked at me with confusion: *what have you done?* But despite the perceived social fall from grace, I never once looked back.

Finding your way in third chakra territory is not about making choices that inflict pain or build a "screw you" attitude, but rather learning to have your own back. Naturally in the kindest, most compassionate way possible, with ahimsa (non-harming) and satya (truth).

The first three chakras include affiliation with earthy things, like your physical body, and are largely concerned with how you relate in your external world; both with others and with yourself.

The last three chakras are where you connect deeply to your spiritual world. The fourth chakra, in a manner of speaking, is where your physicality meets your spirituality. It is the heart chakra, or *Anahata* in Sanskrit, is a vibrant green, and signifies your willingness and ability to follow your heart. Gates often says, "The mind yells; the heart whispers." It's not easy to actually hear what your heart is saying, particularly since we are all bombarded with persuasions to be who we "should" be, so much so that you can become totally out of touch with your inner voice. A voice of kindness and compassion that is innate. Just as it is the nature of the mind to wander, it is the nature of the heart to love. But if you don't slow down and pay attention, you can miss this truism.

The limb of pratyahara is an accessible way to tap into your heart chakra. Get quiet. Go inward. Start the process of interiorization. And then listen, really listen. You might just hear the whisper of your heart. With time and practice, it may get louder. And then you may actually start to live from that place of warmth and open-heartedness towards yourself and others.

Being centered in your heart chakra does not mean that you never have feelings of resentment or negativity towards others. But rather you can become skilled enough to quickly see when you have begun to close your heart. You might notice this as a physical sensation first: a tightness in the chest, a clenching of the jaw. And then once you notice this, you can apply viveka, wise judgment, to assess whether or not you can, or whether or not it is even safe to be open.

Chakra number five is the throat chakra, *Vishuddha* in Sanskrit. It is blue and considered to be the home of communication and self-expression. It captures the idea that what you say is part of your practice. Words matter, a lot. If you want more love and compassion in the world, speak with and be with more love and compassion. As Gandhi said, "Be the change that you wish to see in the world."

The fifth chakra also concerns your ability and willingness to speak your truth. This is where the yama of satya, truthfulness, comes into play. Part of the yoga path is about speaking up for what you believe in. In the face of dissent and opposition, can you say what you mean and mean what you say? And if not, can you inch a little closer to speaking your truth? This is the work you embark on in trying to come into the fifth chakra in a healthy way.

The sixth chakra, *Ajna* in Sanskrit, is located at the third eye center, that space between and above the eyebrows, in the middle of the forehead. This indigo-colored hub is where your intuition and internal wisdom rests. This chakra is where you get really deep into the process of interiorization, meaning not looking for anything outside of yourself to complete you. This is where you come to acknowledge that your happiness does not depend on any external source. There is a kind of detachment that resides here. A letting go of wanting things to be a certain way or not wanting things to be a certain way, and instead stepping into the flow of life that unfolds, moment by moment, with grace and acceptance.

It is easy to get hung up on this idea of detachment. I am not suggesting that you cease caring about your loved ones or striving to obtain life goals. Not at all. But rather to be with what arises; to know that, like everything else in life, it will abide and then dissolve. Then you can more clearly see it with a nonjudgmental, compassionate (third) eye.

When my daughter was a baby, my husband and I considered having another child. To be more precise, I tried to convince him to have another child. I thought I needed another child to feel complete and happy. I thought my daughter needed a little sister or brother to feel complete and happy. My husband—the non-yogi—held my hand, both literally and figuratively, and told me we needed to reach a decision together as a couple.

He insisted that we not simply choose which one of us would get our way. Rather, we needed to process the issue together so that we could reach the same decision about what was best for our family. After a few couples therapy sessions I saw clearly that the right thing was for us to stick with the blessings we had and not add to our family. Our difference in age (my husband is fifteen years older than I), our two older step-kids, and our financial realities all led me to the conclusion that we were good where we were and it really would be best to just focus on nourishing the beautiful family we already had. I also realized I was in an emotionally, physically, and spiritually contracted place by thinking I needed another child to complete me.

My husband's approach was brilliant—it wasn't his way or my way, it was our way. Such a yogi, that one who is nowhere close to ever being able to touch his toes.

For me, this was a tremendous lesson in detachment. When I learned to let go of the result and instead soften into the process my husband had proposed, I was able to expand my heart and mind and be open to what came up. When I did this, I saw the answer with an inner wisdom and clarity. I was practicing detachment, tapping into my third eye chakra, and trusting into the flow of my life.

The seventh chakra, *Sahaswara*, sits at the crown of your head and is considered the physical home of your spiritual enlightenment. Considered to be violet in color, the crown chakra "is our connection to our spiritual nature and our capacity to allow our spirituality to become an integral part of our physical lives and guide us," Myss explains in *Anatomy of the Spirit*. If the root chakra is where you feel grounded and connected to the earth, the crown chakra is where you feel expansive and connected to the whole of the universe. Where you feel into the idea of your interconnectedness. Where you experience the eighth limb of Samadhi.

The chakras can be seen as inherently part of the eight-limbed path of yoga. To begin with, you could experience each of the chakras in every yama and niyama. Looking at the yama of ahimsa (non-violence), by way of example, it is easy to see a natural progression through the chakras. You engage in your root chakra as you survey your relationship to your familial and tribal connections, looking to bring more peace and harmony to them.

As you explore your sacral chakra vis-à-vis ahimsa, you can look to your close personal relationships. Are they rooted in conflict or do they thrive on mutual support and the absence of drama? The yoga path asks you to choose your nearest and dearest carefully, with an eye not only towards your own growth but also towards the growth and well-being of those around you.

Take gossip as just one example. It's all around us, all the time. Many of us do it without even realizing it. Just take a quick look at the magazine racks at the nearest drugstore or airport. They're likely to be replete with gossip-based headlines surmising about who is sleeping with whom, who gained too much weight or who looks unhealthily thin, and who's the best and worst dressed at the latest celebrity shindig.

Gossip is, to put it mildly, extremely hurtful to those caught in its crosshairs. But beyond the obvious damage gossip wreaks on the victim—soiled reputation, broken trust, shame and withdrawal, and more—it's just as damaging to its purveyors. In essence, while they're busy gossiping, they're not tending to their own emotional and spiritual well-being, they're certainly not flexing their compassion muscles, and they're not strengthening positivity loops in their brains.

If you surround yourself with people who gossip, it can be nearly impossible to not get caught up in the riptide. But if you surround yourself with people who cheer you and others on, who support you and others when times are tough, and who work on being their best selves, it's nearly impossible not to be similarly motivated. I strongly encourage you to choose your friends wisely, with much care and attention.

Moving up to the solar plexus chakra, you can explore how well you apply ahimsa to your relationship with yourself. Do you speak to yourself with a compassionate and kind voice or with self-flagellation? Ahimsa insists you cultivate the former. And the practice of yoga in general, and meditation in particular, provides you with helpful tools to first notice your relationship to yourself and then to tend to it with a gentle touch and warm intentions.

The heart chakra is where you might explore your life purpose. The preeminent yoga text, the *Bhagavad Gita*, is largely concerned with how we discern and then live our *dharma*—a powerful Sanskrit term meaning sacred duty or path. Many spiritual traditions, including yoga, are concerned with tapping into and bringing forth our fullest potential during our time on earth. As we hew closer to finding and living our purpose, our dharma, we come into our heart chakras. We also step right into our inner David.

Lest you're feeling overwhelmed or down on yourself for not knowing what your dharma is or how to turn it into your life's work, hang on. We're not talking about winning the Nobel Peace Prize to arrive at your dharma, or finding the cure for cancer or being an Olympic athlete.

Dharma is subtle. It can mean being your best self in all of the areas of your life—in your work cubicle, home, gym, yoga studio, and so on. Maybe your dharma is to make others around you feel loved, accepted, or supported. Perhaps it's to make those you care about laugh. Maybe it's to nurture a beautiful garden and provide refuge for birds and butterflies. Or to feed your family nutritious meals.

There is no end to the list of potential dharmas, and no path is considered too small. Just like a tiny but constant drip of water can carve into a heavy stone, seemingly small acts of love and compassion can carve into a hardened world. So if you're still throwing up your hands in despair because you have no clue about what your dharma is, remember the limb of pratyahara. Get quiet and really listen to your heart. What does it say? You may well find your answer, or get closer to it.

Listening is how I found my way. In 2010 I became interested in the spiritual roots of my Jewish faith. I had a number of close friends who were learning something called mussar, a spiritual practice developed in the Orthodox Jewish community over a thousand years ago. I began to study mussar too, with a beloved teacher who continues to be a spiritual guide for me, and quickly fell in love.

I was at a point in my yoga practice where I felt a little stuck, truth be told. I was years away from even considering becoming a teacher myself and felt like I already knew just about everything in the classes I attended. So mussar entered my life at just the moment I was feeling my yoga path was offering less and less insight and inspiration.

Mussar begins with the premise that we are all spiritual beings who are capable of climbing our own personal growth ladder. It posits that each of us is endowed with a unique cocktail of character traits that makes us who we are. Through the study and practice of mussar, where we explore a series of character traits called "gates" (e.g. the gate of humility, the gate of generosity, etc.), we can refine these traits, bring them into balance, and be our best selves.

I was pretty much hooked from the start. So hooked, in fact, that I began a mussar blog and wrote regularly for about a year. I also went on a women's mission to Israel in 2011 where we intensely explored the spiritual underpinnings of Judaism. Not too long after I got back though, I started a return to my yoga path.

In terms of seeking and finding dharma, I think my exploration of mussar was a near-miss. It was close because it was about personal growth and spiritual development; and I love exploring that. But it was ultimately a miss as my heart was not then, and still is not really involved in Judaism.

It is on the path of yoga where I find my true self. I feel at home on my mat in a way I have never otherwise experienced. I find a sense of inner space that helps me be less reactive and more present when I meditate. I sense an ultimate truth when I study yoga philosophy or work on a particular yama or niyama.

The throat chakra intersects with ahimsa when you examine your speech. Do you speak in a way that causes harm? The third eye chakra is where you can explore the wisdom of compassion-based detachment. Where you can give yourself completely to whatever ahimsa-affirming activities you are engaged in, let go of the results, and trust into the flow of life. When you explore your crown chakra's intersection with ahimsa you can consider leaning into the idea that "We are more alike, my friends, than we are unalike." You can embrace what connects you with all, even in the face of disconnection and dissension.

This chakra-based assessment can be formulated with respect to all of the limbs of yoga.

In a comprehensive asana practice, you can touch on each chakra as part of the progressive flow. For example, in a warrior one pose you can feel into your root chakra; in a balancing dancer pose you can open your heart chakra; and in a camel pose you can access your throat chakra.

In pranayama, you can tap into your root chakra by becoming more grounded and centered.

In pratyahara, you can tap into your heart chakra by exploring the whisper of your heart within.

In dharana, you can focus your mind on one point and thus harness the energy all along your spine to find a connection and an alignment with each of your chakras.

In dhayana, you can practice coming into a deeper meditative state and harnessing the power of your internal wisdom, your third eye chakra.

And in Samadhi, you can find your crown chakra shining brightly as you sit comfortably at home in commitment to your spiritual endeavors.

If you're thinking *Sindy was on to something when she said this chakra stuff might be just a bit too far out there,* don't sweat it. Actually, you don't have to give these energy centers a single thought again if this doesn't resonate with you.

That's part of the beauty of yoga: it is a big-tent offer. I encourage you to partake in asana or pranayama or any of the other limbs of the path that speak to you, and find vitality and peace through them.

CONCLUSION

The ancient tradition of yoga has so much guidance to offer on living your best life and being your best self. By working through the yamas you can refine the way you relate to the world. By working through the niyamas you can tend to yourself in a way that arms you with tools to make wise and compassionate choices. By participating in the practices of asana and pranayama you can tend to your body in a healthy and balanced way. Through the practice of pratyahara you can find refuge from the noise and busyness of modern life. When you practice dharana you can engage your mind in a concerted effort, making it stronger and more focused. Through dhayana you can develop a practice of meditation that strengthens your ability to be mindful and present. And in Samadhi you can realize the truth that you are an integral part of something bigger than yourself.

My journey through the practice of yoga has brought me closer to my best self, my inner David. The path has helped me create a lightness in my life, an openness in my heart, and a presence in my mind. I hope that through your own exploration of the eight-limbed path of yoga, you too will discover a way to cultivate your own inner shine and "radi8" that light out into the world.

Namaste.

ACKNOWLEDGEMENTS

I am filled with gratitude to the teachers who have helped me become the teacher and yogi I am today, and who have imparted wisdom and tools to help me become the teacher and yogi I hope to be tomorrow. Rolf Gates, for your wisdom and for being the incredible teacher that you are. Amy Ippoliti, for your contributions to the world of modern yoga and all things aimed at making the planet a better place. Kim and Scott Curtis, for believing in me and giving me countless opportunities to grow, and for all of the gifts you have given our Yoga Roots community. Sandy Gross, for your wealth of knowledge and for providing me with such a comprehensive platform from which to make the leap from student to teacher. Parker Bean, for showing me the beauty of the path of yoga and for your forever friendship.

Thanks also so much to my friends and family who read early versions of *RADI8* and offered valuable insights and precious time: Susan Stone, Christine Kane, Jennifer Gorman, Amanda Lansman, Heidi Wuescher, and Nancy Lynch. You all pushed me to be a better writer and I am grateful. Thanks too to Lindsay Flack for your beautiful and thoughtful cover design.

To my wonderful stepchildren and their families, Ezra, Danielle, Dante, Penelope, Amanda and Mark. I love you all very much.

And of course to Dan, who lights the way for me every day. Who loves and supports me unconditionally. For being my b'shert and helping me become a better version of myself.

About the Author:

Sindy Warren is an acclaimed yoga and meditation teacher in Cleveland, Ohio. She teaches at Yoga Roots, a yoga studio in Cleveland Heights, Ohio and serves as a Lululemon Ambassador.

In addition to being a yogi, Sindy is an employment lawyer with her own consulting business, Warren & Associates LLC. She incorporates the eight limbs in helping business and managers reach their highest potential.

Sindy lives in Shaker Heights, Ohio with her husband Dan, her daughter Olivia, and her dog Woodrow.

Made in the USA
Columbia, SC
04 September 2018